THE BROWSER'S ECSTASY

Geoffrey O'Brien

The Browser's Ecstasy

A Meditation on Reading

COUNTERPOINT
Washington, D.C.

This book is for
Robert Fagan and Lenore Parker,
friends & readers

Portions of this book, sometimes in different form, have appeared in
Hambone, Michigan Quarterly Review, Open City, and *Word.*

Library of Congress Cataloging-in-Publication Data
O'Brien, Geoffrey, 1948–
The browser's ecstacy : a meditation on reading / Geoffrey O'Brien.
        p.   cm.
        ISBN 1-58243-056-X
    1. Books and reading —Psychological aspects.
        2. Literature—Psychology.   I. Title.
            Z1003.O16   2000
        028'.9—dc21   00-02753

Jacket and text design by Wesley B. Tanner/Passim Editions

Printed in the United States of America on acid-free paper that meets
the American National Standards Institute Z39-48 Standard ∞.

COUNTERPOINT
P. O. Box 65793
Washington D.C. 20035-5793
Counterpoint is a member of the Perseus Books Group

10 9 8 7 6 5 4 3 2 1
FIRST PRINTING

Contents

✳

A Reunion of Old Acquaintances

We had already been talking *about books for several hours.*

It may have been Marjorie who began it, although Rex was quick enough to grab hold of the theme and spin us off into one of his characteristic whimsical flights, in the confidence that the inevitably sober Melchior would bring the talk back to earth. Supper was long since over, and we were sprawled – those of us who had nowhere particular to go and nothing we would rather do than toss about odd anecdotes and random inventions – on the tatty but comfortable armchairs and the single battered sofa in what passed for a sitting room.

The rough weather brewing outside only made us more aware of how delightfully situated we were. It was exactly like a scene in a novel where, mysteriously, none of the characters appears to have any obligations or responsibilities beyond helping the story unfold. Indolently we savored the circulating talk, hanging on the very pauses and momentary hesitations as intently as on the most eloquent outbursts.

It had gotten to that point in any such gathering where the mere fact of talking extends magical possibilities. So magical that even those who refrained almost religiously from speech – the austere Phyllida, for instance, locked in what looked like scornful communion with her cigarette, standing with her back to a sixteenth-century map of Atlantic trade routes – seemed to vibrate to the rapid counter-rhythms of the discussion. From time to time someone got up, paced back and forth in front of the mantelpiece, stooped to refill a glass. The air was smoky and the talk constant, accelerated, a bit too loud at moments.

That we should end up talking about books was almost inevitable. Books were strewn about the room, in no particular order, on the mantel wedged between bookends shaped like men-at-arms, piled up promiscuously on side tables, gathering dust in corners; one (an economics textbook with a torn cover) had been jammed against the door to keep a draft from creeping in. No telling how many decades some of those books had been in the room: one by one they had washed up, books of no particular interest to anyone and hence abandoned to a common space. There was a guide (sadly out of date) to the restaurants and entertainments of Toronto and vicinity; a detective novel by an industrious but none too inspired imitator of Agatha Christie; a monograph likening certain legends of Micronesia to the structure of certain experimental novels; a study of the inner life of mid-level managers that had made considerable impact when published in the immediate aftermath of the Suez crisis; a slim but dauntingly opaque treatise called simply Thoughts as Objects; and, flung carelessly in a corner (the one

A Meditation on Reading

item that appeared to have been read in full and repeatedly), a thick paperback with a torn cover on which a buxom adventuress and a brawny adventurer posed against a collage of palm trees, schooners, and glittering ballrooms. All in all it was an average catch of Gutenbergian flotsam.

What, in any case, could have been more natural to us than to talk about books? We were bookish people, steeped in a conversation about books that had already lasted years. We had read so many novels that our lives (our lives being definable as what became of us in the intervals between reading novels) had themselves inevitably become a sort of messy open-ended novel. The space between the novels we read and the novel we lived was a zone of cunningly sustained indeterminacy where we were free to meditate on the reciprocity linking the rejected lover drowned in the pond and the anxious vacation à trois, the fatal letter of denunciation and the missed train on Monday morning, the plague on the estate and the disastrous dinner party, the foreign invasion and the stymied promotion, the masked ball interrupted by madness and the badminton match interrupted by an unusually brisk August breeze. Was it not a system of reflections, of imitations so subtle that the observer could hardly tell which was the model and which the copy?

Books went from hand to hand among us. With the exchange of a book many a love affair had begun; with a sudden change of opinion about the merits of a particular book had been signaled many a rupture of relations. At times one or another of us had found a book truly superior, capable of absorbing and replacing all

3

the rest of them, and this had led to many chilling disagreements, to fierce and sometimes nearly violent rejoinders. There were regrets and denunciations; beloved books that were finally found unworthy; despised books in whose pages hidden riches were at length discovered. Sometimes these things had to be worked out chapter by chapter, sentence by sentence. And how many unuttered curses and unresolved quarrels had been relegated to the margins of the kind of book in which it was still permissible to challenge one's enemy to a duel, or to hire assassins among the riffraff of the rue Saint-Lazare?

But all that was years ago. What was broken off with books had later been joined together again with books. Subsequent chapters emended and elaborated what earlier chapters had recklessly truncated and defaced. Through books we felt we lived multiple existences not precisely our own, lives of monastic austerity or courtly riot or flyblown squalor. To talk about those books, those lives, was a further interweaving that made them even more profoundly part of us.

We would, surely, have been quite lost without them. Yet when we talked about them it felt oddly like talking about nothing at all, like talking about weather or furniture. Tonight, for instance: no reason to believe that this discussion would have any more decisive consequences than the thousand and one discussions that had preceded it. We did not look to any impending resolution; we simply continued.

The Demon

A FEW MOMENTS EARLIER *our talk had taken a peculiar turn. Melchior had muttered something about "the eternal figure of the demon who wants to destroy all books," and the phrase had set us off into a somewhat giddy expansion of its implications. Where did the demon come from? Our words had invented him, and now we were stuck with him. For the moment we wanted to be stuck with him: with such a demon in view, our conversation was raised from a minor parlor game to a confrontation with the end of all things. He was an emblem, this demon, of everything that books could neither encompass nor control. He gave our talk some edge: a hint of anxiety that the books, and their readers with them, might after all prove a mouthful for this great devourer.*

— Nothing like a bit of apocalyptic dread to lend savor to the passing moment, Marjorie observed.

— Think of him (said Rex) as the undying and malevolent genius who haunts marches and outlands, war tents and back alleys, raging to erase whatever passes beyond his control. Thousands upon thousands of swarming stanzas and story lines. Genealogies

and catechisms. Jokes, epithets, slogans, riddles. He stomps on the epic and the proverb escapes from between his toes. He silences the hymn and gets drowned out by the laughter provoked by the ribald tale they're telling in the alley behind the cathedral. He burns all the novels only to find that the burning has itself become the subject of a novel, and himself its unforgettably caricatural protagonist. It isn't fun being an annihilator, he gets downright depressed. He can almost believe he will be written out of existence, that the history of the world will be his failure writ large: the by now ridiculous story of his bungled attempt to erase history.

– Even the demon (Philip chimed in) acknowledges that power: after all, for every book he burns, he substitutes a lookalike. You know the sort of thing, looks like a book, has paragraphs and plots like a book, argues and even sometimes amuses like a book, but somehow you know just from the way the cover feels or the choice of typeface – not to mention the paper! – that it's a sort of placebo. If it amuses, it isn't from any solicitude for the reader's pleasure, but for reasons of strategy. Its only purpose is to preempt the place of other books and thus keep people from reading them. There are whole nations full of them, books that pretend to be irresistible like an invitation to a lawn party when in fact they're irresistible like a visit from the secret police.

– We, on the other hand (said Rex), help keep things real, I suppose. Help keep them together. Keep the dialogue going.

He paused for a moment, then resumed:

– We create the haven by which we're sheltered, whose walls

are woven of allusions and cross-references. (*Here he caressed, as if by way of example, a few battered books of Roman history that lay by the side of the armchair, odd volumes of Dio Cassius in the Loeb Classics edition.*) Four thousand years make a thick braid. And the ashes of the books that were burned form a sort of lime or cement to bind it thicker.

— Yes (*said Andrea, at vehement speed*), and the rewritings, the synopses of the lost books — the quotations from which the contents of vanished libraries may be surmised — the thirdhand half-remembered reconstructions of whole systems of philosophy — tragedies glimpsed phantasmally in imitations of imitations of the destroyed texts: every piece of learned hearsay tightens the knots. "Once upon a time there was a story." Once it is written down, the faintest echo or rumor adds precious strength to the defensive perimeter. If it isn't written down, of course, it might as well never have been.

— It's as if we're inside this thing that's ever so much larger than us, part of an endless process of transmission, with all sorts of embellishments and design changes along the way but with something fundamental preserved despite everything. It's positively . . . genetic. Sort of like eternity except that it never stops being interesting.

— But you've got it all wrong (*one among us interjected*).

We turned in astonishment toward the corner from which he had spoken.

A Mysterious Disappearance

HE HAD NOT PREVIOUSLY SPOKEN. *We had not really known he was there. In a curious way he seemed a stranger – I think each of us assumed he must be a friend of someone else's friend – even though he must have been among us from the start, since no one had entered or left the room. We were thrown off balance. There was an uncomfortable sense of having been spied on. Beyond that, we had begun to intuit that however much this stranger might know about us by now – whatever he had gathered by sitting among us and soaking up our talk – we could somehow never come to know anything at all about him.*

The rhythm was broken. We settled into a restive silence as he continued to speak. His voice had a curious undertone of conviction, of warning almost.

– I mean, this thing you imagine you're inside may already have ceased to exist.

Someone ventured, with a timidity that was new to us, that this was a rather absurd proposition.

– Not at all, *said the stranger.* It takes time for things to become known, and by the time you've found out – well, you might already be gone.

Another among us allowed that he did not care for the sound of all this. It was enough to give one the creeps. What, he ventured, was the idea? Was our very existence to be called into question?

– You see (*resumed the speaker*) it *has* already ended. I've seen it as clearly as I see you. A new space has been created, unimaginable to you just as you are unimaginable within it. It's a space in which the idea of your life doesn't exist. The books have not been burned but displaced, carted away to a remote site for storage purposes. The process was so gradual that no one can say exactly when the removal got under way or at just what point it became irrevocable.

(Just as irrevocably, we continued to listen, sensing that from this point on we would no longer be able to say a word in rejoinder. This stranger – who was somehow at the same time our intimate, since he had sat in our midst – exercised impalpable dominion over our impulses. We began to feel that in an obscure way we depended on him; if he stopped talking the whole lot of us, and the room we were gathered in, might flick off like a light.)

It wasn't a high-intensity purge; no one felt threatened. More like a design decision. Without much apparent discussion, a consensus was arrived at, the acknowledgment of a pervasive loss of interest. If any debate took place, it was so muted – so specialized and marginal – that hardly anyone noticed when it stopped. They cleared out the volumes with as little interest or enthusiasm as a custodian tidying up a waiting room, removing outdated issues of *TV Guide* and *Dental Health Today*, newsletters from state senators, announcements from local department stores of back-to-school sales.

Picture it. All the rooms have been cleaned out. As a concept for interiors it's bracing: Empty Chic. The surfaces of desks and shelves and tables assume a bristling unimpeded power they were never imagined to possess, an almost overpowering straightforwardness. What frankness! The rooms exhibit a raw force that (as it seems in retrospect) had been subdued or obscured by those piles of books – books read or half-read in decades past, or purchased with a view to being read in future decades that never quite arrived – faint reminders of a vanished excitement (the incomparable excitement of being on the verge of opening a book one wants to read), or promises finally recognized as unlikely to be fulfilled. After the books sat there long enough, they weren't even visible. They squatted in the field of vision – smudged, flaking, splitting, coated with dust – like the residue of hopes virtually evaporated.

What did the books do, except deflect, or intrude, or simply obstruct?

Face it: they had become a sort of eyesore, a visual nuisance. They were statues of bygone thoughts, photographs of ancestors that no one could quite remember, insistent ghosts turning truculent when they realized they could no longer frighten anyone. They tended to soften or undercut the sense of immediacy.

Merely by their presence they implied something beyond the room, something deeper or older that would explain the room, ratify the room. They were a continual taunting reminder of things not done, paths not followed, customs no longer honored, histories no longer remembered. They made the room itself oddly threadbare and inadequate.

Once they have been extracted from space, it becomes possible to perceive a world of naked structures, girders, scaffolding, strips of hooks, the jagged and shimmering desert to which the books had imparted a veneer of coziness. Henceforth explanations are in plain view or they are nowhere.

As far as I can make out, this has already happened, even if you haven't registered it yet.

A Night Journey

AND IN THE AFTERMATH of making that realization, I dreamt I felt my way in the dark until I found the warehouse where the vanished books were stowed. This was last night. I say "I dreamt" because there isn't any other way I can explain it in your language, but it was no dream. When I was in your midst, sharing your talk, it was as if all things were linked, as if we passed through communicating doors into a common room whose elements—all those books for instance – were part of a single thing, a single world. It was a human world: everything in it seemed to have been designed by someone who cared. Out here, by contrast – out here where you can never join me – things stand on their own, external and broken up. There are rough changes of weather, unsettling changes of scene. You can't count on anything to mean something in the way a sentence means something. It's different in a way for which neither you nor your books could ever offer adequate preparation.

To find the books in such a place – the very books that you've been making so much of – was the coldest touch of all. The books weren't there to be preserved, merely to endure a slow death, a little bit slower than ours. I can still picture that drafty half-decayed place, that cavernous interior snaking on for miles. By nothing more than intuition I make my way inside. It's completely black, and thick with objects. The only meaningful problem is to find a light source, a lamp or flashlight by which to scan the titles of the volumes, or at least those that are still readable, that have not already crumbled or been eaten by insects.

It would be worth the whole world, I imagine, for a momentary beam to illumine a single page, a portion of a single page, a phrase, a word. As if in response, a flash of indeterminate origin – aurora borealis? searchlight? effect of a distant explosion? – allows me to glimpse one fragment: I try to read by the afterglow. But whatever was usable in the flash has already been swallowed up in the ungenerous dark.

It seems horrible that the sentence thus caught sight of should be permitted neither start nor end, nothing but that rising curve in the middle – "said that the sky" or "and is to rain when" or "which parted further to let" – and then truncation. Signal gone dead. Sitting in the dark, I try to find a way to tug at the surviving fragment in order to find the sentence it was attached to. It seems a purely physical task, like threading a needle or hauling in the survivors of a foundered boat. You get the hook in and yank the sentence out, and then once you have the sentence you can pull on it to draw out more and more of the web of which it's only a single strand.

In the absence of light, it's solely by force of thought that I can hope to read a book that has already become invisible. It becomes an article of faith that the passage somewhere continues to go on; that while the reader may end, the book never does; that by reading I insinuate myself into a continuity; and that . . .

The Warehouse

And then I wake up. Only of course it's just another part of the dream, a familiar leap into the next episode. It's the kind of dream where everything is all too real, where objects are reconstituted with oppressive fidelity, as if to demonstrate what a good observer the brain is even when it seems to be idling. Yes, that's exactly what a paper-cup dispenser looks like. Radiators have just such knobs.

I'm in a motel room with no books, only a shuttered darkness and some strips of pale fluorescent tubing by which it would be impossible to read, if there were anything to read except the shifting pressure fronts of the Weather Channel. The television seems to have turned itself on automatically; perhaps it was never off, just snoozing in standby mode. The arrows and bands of color permit me to read the ambient air mass as a purposeful discourse, a communiqué about what direction the day is moving in. The announcement goes by so quickly and then disappears beyond recall: "What did he say the weather was going to be?"

The voice reading headlines on the news has the intensity of a privileged and solitary heat source. Without books, it's the only gate by which words are permitted to issue, a shoulder over which no one can look to peek at the script he's reading from. I hadn't thought it possible to return so completely to the childish condition of being read to, of receiving in illiterate gratitude whatever fragments of story are doled out.

I have been delivered from reading books so that I can spend the day reading other things. Taking things in the proper spirit – with suitable optimism – it becomes possible to make almost a religion of illiteracy. How good for the soul it might be to study milk diffusion on the surface of the coffee cup, to read the aspect of the sky at street level while walking to the car and, as the car moves along the thruway, to read color and density of vegetation and surmise what time of year it is. No books, and therefore nothing that is not to be read, nothing that the eye can afford to neglect in case it harbors a message. The world is a big naked book, the book that books concealed.

I'm wondering if I can get used to this, can even learn to enjoy it.

But I mustn't let this huge bare world distract me from my mission. My purpose – somehow I just know this, nobody told me – is to infiltrate the warehouse where the books have been deposited. There is something there I urgently need to know, even if it is the knowledge of what I lack, which it is essentially too late to make up for. I know intimately the region where the warehouse is concealed. Didn't I spend part of my childhood there, wasn't it indeed in childhood, the first time I ever laid eyes on a book, that I had an inkling of everything that has since come to pass?

A road (the dream reminded me of it) leads there circuitously. Just past the Fallen Rock Zone, the thruway deviates into a local turnpike. The turnpike curves into a narrow and heavily forested lane that will in turn without warning become a dirt path, practically a gully. The barnlike structure beyond will be invisible from even a few hundred yards away.

On the other hand, maybe I've never seen this place before. Maybe the childhood I remember has been implanted (but by whom?), in the same way that one can fall in love in a dream with a fictive being, and wake filled with melancholy love-longing over the absence of someone who never existed. So the books I go to recapture (the books I seem to remember having read in childhood) may turn out when I finally examine them to be volumes never before opened, a record of utterly and disruptively strange messages. They will tell me that the life I thought I led was a sort of interim or suspension; that real life, all along, was transpiring in secret within the closed book.

On the road to the invisible warehouse, I find in my surroundings everything that could be imagined as readable, except a face. I am alone: that is a further condition of the journey. Sky and bushes and asphalt become, in compensation, a succession of faces. The landscape looks back at me. The roadway narrows expressively as it loops into the mountain bend, as if broaching a transition into a new chapter. As on a chart I trace the progression of the sun across the horizon and the attendant darkening of the roadway. In the white flat sky I read imminence of untimely frost; I read progressive distance from any home I have ever had; I read arrival at the remote outpost where the past is waiting, the place where the books are hidden.

I'm moving closer toward what already happened, toward an origin that can reveal nothing but my own helplessness. In just the same way, on beginning a book, the reader finds only the past, only what is already written down, lying in wait like a lion carved out of stone.

The door, when I'm finally in front of it, is also, as always, like a book not yet opened. It promises something known and strange, the same old place where something certifiably different will always be happening, or else a place encountered for the first time where nonetheless familiar events will recur (it is never clear at the outset whether the events will be soothingly or disturbingly familiar). So do the books tell only of familiar things, familiar births, massacres, floods, reincarnations, courtroom interrogations, love triangles, bank failures, plagues, telephone calls – even familiar surprises, familiar anomalies, familiar miracles.

Land Without Seasons

I'VE GONE INSIDE, I'm in the building. It's a different order of space. Whatever clutter was removed from the world
outside, to make its lines cleaner and its functioning more
efficient, has washed up inside these walls. If everything I
want isn't here, there is at least a record of everything I
might want, or at any rate that anyone might once have
wanted. If it isn't written here it isn't written anywhere, it
isn't writable.

Having found the source, there remains the question of
what I can possibly hope to accomplish here. I can look
around and try to get a sense of what's on hand, and remember as much as I can, inventing the parts I can't remember, imagining the parts I can't invent. If I'm an agent,
on whose behalf? Do I need to report back to a headquar-
ters I cannot now (in this dimensional frame) quite concep-
tualize? To undergo a debriefing in which I will recapitulate
as best I can everything that was stored there, translating
every detail into terms they will understand, whatever terms
they require for their essentially unknowable purposes? For

that purpose I need to decide what I have seen, what I am seeing.

It's important to give names to all the things I see and then figure out a way to remember the names, some mode of listing.

My first impulse, however, is to do nothing at all. The books are impressive even without being opened. The sight of them has the weight of elephants or temple complexes or mountain ranges. I could be a shepherd staring blankly at distant rock formations, knowing nothing of the names of the peaks or the people who inhabit them.

Portions of covers are visible in the heaps: gold letters on purple, red letters on white, yellow letters on black, a priest in his alb, a woman with a martini glass, tugboats and skyscrapers, a solitary tractor, stars and splotches and polka dots and wavy lines. Fragments of titles cry out, like voices choked off in mid-yell: *National* — *River* — *Of Delight* — *Formation* — *They Came* — *Ivory* — *A Life* — *Fundamentals* — *And Smoke* — *Made Easy* — *In the Bronze* — *Prisoners*.

It begins to rain suddenly and heavily. The downpour releases the sleeping odors of the empty farm building, a rich heritage of must and corruption. It does not abate, it thickens to a new density and urgency, an aroma palpable enough to pass for a population. What's out the window is erased by the torrent. A blank slate: wobbly blur through which the underlying green gleams and recedes as if inhaling and exhaling. The sibilance and clatter distance me further from whatever is outside this shell. Beyond the door, all is roar and disorder, no place for a person to take shelter.

My universe is reduced to an island of abandoned furniture and tools, darts, hinges, crushed Ping-Pong balls, broken phonograph records, frames from which the photographs have been removed, and the boxes and loose stacks of old books set adrift in a storm. In a short while they too will be removed, since putting things in storage is generally a prelude to destroying them altogether. It's a kind of trial separation to see if it is possible to live without them. That will leave the building entirely empty except for the ghosts of those who might once actually have read these books, ghosts whose whispering is drowned out by the concert of the winds.

I will open a book in a moment. Not quite yet. I want to savor the hiatus between catching sight of and catching hold of, between opening the eyes and seeing. After all, it is a terrible thing to open a book. Who knows what might fly in my face, what private quarrel I might interrupt, or what battlefield casualties I might stumble over?

A palsied gypsy woman will hurl threats across the page. A vengeful sea dog will pass me the Black Spot. I will be compelled to look at some sacrificial Olmec ritual or misguided episode of seventeenth-century jurisprudence, images which can never thereafter be erased. A thought will be planted with whose harvest I will henceforth have to live on intimate terms. I will wonder, years later, if my life would have been quite different if I had not, on such and such a day, opened a certain book to a certain page.

If there were a narrative that could clarify my situation to me, how might it go? A man finds his way back to a room in which are sequestered all the books he has ever read and all he ever wanted to read and all whose possibility he ever imagined. (He had attempted systematically to imagine all possible books in the hope of stumbling by chance across an impossible one.) His task – imposed he cannot quite know by whom, or toward what end – is to sort through what's in the room; to steep himself in whatever he can, as long as he can, as in an occult bath. How it is to be gauged at what point he will have attained optimum absorption is a problem yet to be worked out. He feels, indeed, as if he were still laying groundwork, still making rough notes toward the terms in which that problem might be formulated. The time available for making such a formulation is not indefinite. This is one of those places where you are not permitted to abide forever. They close it on you when you least expect it.

Light leaks from the sky but has not yet been replaced entirely by the blackness biding its time. As for other conventional signs of the natural world – cicada chirps or the creaking of icicles suspended from roof gutters or dry leaves blown scraping along the pavement or the competitive croaks of bullfrogs in chorus along the pond's edge – not a hint. No season lives here. This space has quite successfully shut out any such interference. The cunning designer saw to it that there is not even a mirror in which the reader might contemplate his own appearance or anxiously search for the marks of age. The climate is grammatical. Nothing here but books, as if I were swaddled in them, as if the porous walls of books were by now almost a second skin. Or as if they provided a padding like the walls of madhouses, a cushion constructed of the language of the dead.

Lumber Room

"LANGUAGE OF THE DEAD": technically, this is not quite accurate, since some of the authors of some of the books are of course still living. But whether they are living or not is beside the point. Once a book exists, it takes its place indistinguishably among the writings of the dead. The words have been fixed, never to move again except in the mind of a reader. Readers, on the other hand, unlike authors, must be alive in order to fulfill their function.

In the presence of so much yellowing printed matter I feel not only alive but refreshed. A fathomless appetite stirs. I almost literally crawl among the books as if crawling around the storeroom off the garage attached to a house where I stayed once. It's a space the way spaces used to be, before the first encounter with the letters of the alphabet. I remember now how space tumbled open at every step, and by virtue of that memory it continues to do so. In that cobwebbed kingdom the rows of books were like rows of cupboards with rusty handles, each to be tried in turn: What's in this one, or this one?

A Meditation on Reading

It was a ramshackle lumber room where odd tools were to be found, sawed-off fragments of carpentry, rags and sandpaper, bolts and nails buried in sawdust, sheets of yellowed newspaper lining shelves: *Truman to intervene in labor dispute, Father tells why he killed daughter's husband, Waiter fined five dollars in restaurant brawl.* A moldy treasury came piecemeal to the surface, by the light of a crudely rigged bare bulb. Here it was, the hidden book, the lost book, the discarded book, its cover rotted, its pages loose, crammed in a supply closet or fallen behind a heavy table: *Basic Principles of Electricity, Our Singing World, Janet Hardy in Hollywood, You Must Relax!*

Reading matter. Catalogues, children's encyclopedias, religious pamphlets, government-issued health and safety manuals. Calendars on which a beautiful girl held up a stein of beer or an elk stooped to drink from a mountain stream or a Biblical prophet cast angry glances in the direction of a gem-encrusted idol. A price guide for rock collectors, the rules for a lost board game, a book club bulletin announcing a historical novel set during the era of Reconstruction. Mildewed copies of magazines with names like *Pep* and *Zip*. A quiz book called *What Do You Know?* full of questions about Knute Rockne and "Wrong Way" Corrigan, the Herman Rosenthal murder and the Teapot Dome scandal and the *Shenandoah* dirigible disaster. A foldout collection of postcards from the Texas Centennial Exposition of 1936, featuring a moonlit view of the Tower of Religion. A cluster of blue-covered booklets on sex hygiene, social revolution, the lives of Balzac and Jack London, and the agnostic doctrines of Robert Ingersoll. The complete blank verse text of a pageant staged in Central Park on the quadricentennial of America's discovery. A nineteenth-century manual of diseases and abnormalities of the hair and scalp, full of meticulous and unspeakable engravings. A military phrasebook teaching how to say "Throw down your weapon" in every major European language. Finally, a handful of outmoded books on current affairs – *You Can't Do Business with Hitler, One World, Victory Through Air Power* – roughly wedged in place to prop up a wobbly workbench.

Legacy from Space

From the memory of those surroundings I can reconstruct clearly how it felt to have just grasped what the alphabet was. The moment of apprehending that the mark spoke – that the letter represented a sound – was unspeakable. It was the birth of an intimacy. The child who learns to read is a master of voices – or is he mastered by voices? A privacy (never once thought of as such until the instant it ended) was irrevocably broken in upon. Now that the books on the shelf were known to hum with thought, thought could never again be solitary, if it ever had been.

Once upon a time I began where I will end, at a moment probably quite like this one, in a room lined with books. Four walls marked the four cardinal directions, certifying that this was a sealed world harboring all necessary coordinates. That original book room is now an idea that I can summon up effortlessly, but it was once just a physical location; in the same way that letters were once black marks instead of ideas. Have I been trying ever since to reverse the process, and turn the words and ideas back into marks and

spaces? I caught a glimmer of how irrevocable those trans-
formations were at the moment when I had just learned to
decipher the titles on the shelves. The logic was immutable:
If there are books, then there must be a room in which the
books exist. This is a book, and therefore it exists in a room,
this room; the room is in a house; I live in the house; the
house is in the world, therefore there is a world, which, ar-
guing by extension, I inhabit.

How evident it was, in the first childish survey of the
shelves, that space creatures had come and abandoned their
works behind them. No reading could ever surpass for sheer
strangeness that first encounter with the names of books: to
make out the names of doors into the unknown, with no
hint of their meaning. They could have been *anything*. The
outer space visitors had left as a token of their visit only this
wall of spines, of road signs. Any one of them might as well
have borne the title of one of the Agatha Christie paper-
backs: *Destination Unknown*.

The fundamental shock of reading was the initial deci-
phering. The power of the titles lay in their pristine, un-
compromised mysteriousness: *The Cream of the Jest. The
Crock of Gold. Shining Trumpets. Hot Countries. Blood in the
Streets. Apples and Madonnas. The Fall of a Titan. The Touch of
Nutmeg Makes It. The Tribe That Lost Its Head. The Bible as
History. The Idea of a Theatre. With Malice Toward Some. The
End of All Men. When the Mountain Fell. The Descent of Man. A*

A Meditation on Reading

Family of Engineers. Generation of Vipers. Burning Bright. A Pin to See the Peepshow. Good Night, Sweet Prince. Try and Stop Me. The Sun Is My Undoing. The Sea and the Jungle. A Crystal World. The Purple Land. The titles could be read but not understood; the purpose of reading the book, when it came time for that, would be to understand at last what the title meant. But could any book live up to the infinite suggestiveness of those arcane tags?

Unlike toothbrushes or bugles or vacuum cleaners, these objects had no obvious use. The neutral observer stood contemplating how and for what end the marks were made. Why would a particular slant go one way rather than another? On a foreign highway, at an obviously crucial crossroads, the traveler comes upon a sign in an unknown alphabet. Perhaps the sign is there to warn him of danger, or to direct him toward food and shelter, or to provide him with a choice between two antithetical nations along whose border he is unwittingly wandering, or to inform him that beyond a certain point no road exists.

BEFORE ANY POSSIBILITY OF MEANING, there was a brutal face-to-face meeting. Eyes and letters stared each other down in an otherwise empty world. Limit encountered limit. In the space between, the birth of desire occurred. What other choice was there than to breach the apparent barrier and walk into the new country? The reader let his eyes wander over the illegible complexity of the signs with the impatient curiosity of a famished traveler suddenly catching sight of a tavern sign creaking above hedgerows, or of a pirate surveying the harbor and skyline of the city he is preparing to sack.

The desire was to climb as literally as possible up into those syllables, as into a house among the trees. The Forest of Arden is made of words, and there was never a better forest, nor was there ever a better purple, a better jungle, a better fall, a better theater. Written language was a plank extending from the shore where they make planks, the distant city of the word-founders.

The plank, a path over a void, leads toward the next part of the plank. One word opens the way for the next word: handholds in a rock face. The mind clambers among them, looking first for a toehold, then for the serious ledge that will allow it to get up and over. At any given moment a single word may have to bear the full load of someone digging his toe or heel into it for dear life. I come to know them by leaning and gripping. Each word forms part of an intimate relief map of traction and slippage. This one you can safely press against; over yonder the ground is apt to give way unexpectedly. There are trails that ice over undetectably at the first frost.

That the clambering is never completed, the opening never altogether cleared, is its charm. It always leaves some ground still to be crossed. The reader, in his mortal vanity, will not deign to recognize a cutoff point. No arrival: the valley simply extends and thickens, and I proceed, I become part of it or it becomes part of me. The text will persist, and by reading it I become part of the text in a way that curiously evades the imprisonment of past or future.

Prisoners

THE HORROR WOULD BE to have read all that was written, to have come to the end of books: a horror that prisoners and soldiers know, parceling out their few available books page by page, a page a day so as to last out the year. The American taken prisoner by the Germans was told that he would be given one book a week, selected at random by his jailers: the world would be heaven or hell depending on whether the book was a novel by John Galsworthy or a manual of chemical elements, the life of Julian the Apostate or a directory of the Shriners of Luzerne County, Pennsylvania.

The prisoner in Stefan Zweig's *The Royal Game* saw salvation from his solitary imprisonment by the Gestapo in the book he was able to smuggle into his cell, without having any idea of its nature until he was finally alone with his prize:

> The mere idea of a book in which words appear in orderly arrangement, of sentences, pages, leaves, a book in which one could follow and stow in one's brain new, unknown, diverting thoughts was at once intoxicating and stupefying. . . . I wanted, first of all, to savour the joy of possessing

A *Meditation on Reading*

a book; the artificially prolonged and nerve-inflaming desire to day-dream about the kind of book I would wish this stolen one to be.

It turned out, to his initial horror, to be an anthology of chess games: something that could not be read at all without mastering a hitherto alien language. Through absorption in those diagrams, the prisoner would in the end explore the outer limits of monomania, literally driven mad by his involuntary choice of reading matter.

I prefer to believe that somewhere in this heap of books there is one I cannot imagine. The unread book is the life yet to be lived, the promise that there will be new ideas, images never yet glimpsed. The paradise of futurity is the thousand-page book full of episodes still to come: a book of mysteries disguised as a mystery book with an inexplicably alluring title, *The Secret of the Desert* or *The Adventure of the Lost Key*.

Key to All Keys

But FIRST IT MUST BE FOUND. There is another horror, of inaccessibility. The thing exists but I can't locate it, can't put it in front of me. Perhaps years of search, a lifetime, would be enough to track it down. Ask the others. Somebody may know. Or they may misunderstand and send me exactly the wrong way. I must eat the road as I travel it, so that only after digesting half the world – reading half the library – will I find that tiny corner I was so desirous, at the outset, of locating.

There is a paralysis, a despair. Everything is too far away. It seems too immense, somehow, even to lift a finger. The weight of the years and the words exceeds the tiny strength one is allotted. To read two or three sentences is already a terrible labor. Simply to dip into these waters is overwhelming; but to navigate them, to find a particular island in them, spills over into the realm of the heroic.

Why not then simply admire the heroes, the omnivores, the memorious scholars and vatic connoisseurs who return from far distances with the gleam of the incommunicable in their eyes? They are devoured by what they devour; the path eats them. It took a lifetime to find, in the air, the link between two apt quotations that lay buried two thousand years apart from each other. With a smile of something resembling satisfaction, the by now ancient doctor watches the evidence fall into place, in the form of a telltale anachronism of syntax: just as expected, but it is gratifying to find confirmation.

One could, of course, just as easily spend a lifetime walking in the wrong direction. A map would help; one could even spend that same lifetime reading nothing but maps, staring entranced at networks of routes. In the same spirit, the reader looks at catalogues of titles, watching from his inviolable perch as eras disgorge their novels and treatises and histories, so numerous that in the end what is needed is not a catalogue but a catalogue of catalogues.

Nets have been cast to prevent anything from escaping. The catch is piled up encyclopedically, so that the eye at a glance can scan centuries of battles, genealogies of titleholders, generations of sequels. People have gone to a great deal of trouble to condense what is known to manageable proportions, to make sure that no salient point gets passed over. It would at any rate be pleasant to imagine that they have gone to a great deal of trouble. That way you would not be afraid of being misled, of missing the most important sights. The eye is in a hurry. There are only so many years for rummaging through the basement, only so many hours when the light is good enough. The hand, groping impatiently in clutter and dust, seeks (against all reasonable expectation) to lay hold of a Key to All Keys.

The Book of Knowledge

IN CHILDHOOD – somebody's childhood – there had been *The Book of Knowledge,* a monument in twenty-odd red-covered volumes of late imperial upbringing, preserving intact the world undone by the Great War. Here was kept alive, as if in some sealed attic, that long and ponderous peace in which knowledge consisted of juxtaposed episodes from Roman history, exercises in French conversation, beloved scenes from Dickens, playlets for schoolchildren, lessons in knitting and penmanship and map reading, magic tricks, secrets of nature and the body, résumés of the history and geography of the great countries and cities. Here, if anywhere, was the paradise of randomness. Everything made sense, in any order whatsoever. The world was a loose assembly of coherences: silkworms, gold mines, eclipses, thermometers, viaducts. And there were worlds within worlds: "We should almost think of the soap bubble as made of millions and millions of tiny little creatures, each with its arms all around it, and all these arms holding on to the arms round them."

No book ever asked more profound questions. They were scattered throughout its volumes in bold black type, each time waking the reader to some fresh apprehension: Why Can We Not Walk Straight with Our Eyes Shut? Are There More People Coming Into the World Than Going Out of It? Will the World's Food Supply Ever Run Short? Could We Live Without Rain? How Are Burglars Caught by Fingerprints? Why Does a Stick Hold Together? Can a Fish Hear? What Brings Life Out of Dried Seeds? Where Does Music Come From? Why Do Some Faces in Pictures Seem to Follow Us? Do We See What Is Not There? How Big Is the World?

And in the place where the answers were supposed to be – under, say, the rubric The Meaning of Words – were more questions: "Have you ever wondered why one word means one thing and another word means something quite different? Isn't it funny that BREAD never means CHEESE? Why doesn't it? Why was bread called bread, and cheese called cheese?" Yet the question could hardly trouble, since so many answers were lying around. Anything the eye fell on was an answer merely by virtue of existing: the medicine dance of the Winnebago Indians, the most beautiful library in the world, the five hundred kinds of hummingbirds, the stream of water constantly flowing through the body.

The surest answer was the past, spread out in luxurious invitation. How busy they were in the past! Peter the little

A Meditation on Reading

Dutch boy shoring up the leak in the dike and Gaius Mucius Scaevola holding his hand in the flame, Sir Walter Raleigh spreading his cloak to prevent Queen Elizabeth from stepping into a mud puddle, Robert the Bruce watching the spider spin its web, Alfred the Great letting the farm woman's cakes burn, Pope Leo eyeing the British barbarians being sold into slavery and exclaiming "They are not Angles but Angels," a German monk inventing gunfire, Joan of Arc urging on the French troops at Orleans, Saint Patrick driving the snakes from Ireland, William Tell taking aim at the apple on his son's head, the Swiss Guards massacred holding off the revolutionary mob at the Tuileries, Ethan Allen and the Green Mountain Boys overrunning Fort Ticonderoga, Pickett leading his last mad charge at Gettysburg. You may fire when you are ready, Gridley – don't fire until you see the whites of their eyes – damn the torpedoes – I have not yet begun to fight. Catherine the Great is in the room, President Garfield is in the room. There is only the one instant, in which knowledge occurs.

Family Romance

I BEGIN TO REMEMBER how a child reads, as if the characters were his family and the settings his hometown. Every tree and every stick of furniture is supplied from those around him. My brother discovered Venezuela! My sister poisoned the Pope! My uncle was the president of the Nebraska Cattlemen's Association! All my cousins lived on a remote plantation on the steppes and their lives were interrupted by edicts and rebellions.

For the child, every description leads back toward what is in front of his senses. The novel is a history of his attention span. He sits in the room where the scene takes place, inhabits the baron or the traitor like a wandering demon. Then, having peopled the book with his family, he recasts the family as a book. The family acts out the story of the book within which the story of the family is inscribed. With eyes closed or open, book open or shut, he reads and reads.

To read like the child would be to approach the book once again with fear. A new chapter is dangerous. There is no protection from the shock of the characters' speech, the bare outrageousness of their curses, their sorrow. The sentence is larger than life, almost as big as the mind of the person reading it. The least pronouncement resounds universally.

The eyelash of the girl in the Pushkin poem is gigantic. The phrases are enormous chunks of sculpture, weightlessly penetrating space. In the Henry James novel the tiny tremblings of sensibility rear up ponderous and ungainly, suspended as if over an abyss, in a corner of the sitting room. A year passes in the interval since she tilted her head away from the lamp, perhaps to conceal a fleeting look of anxiety. The description of space, in Dickens or James, seems to dilate in order to admit shifting quantities of light and shadow, to expose a hidden three-dimensionality. To look into the words is to look into a literal space. He chooses a book as he would choose a room to hole up in: or cave, or mesa, or hidden vantage point among the giddy crisscrossing alleys of the modern city.

Miniatures

A BOX WITH THE WORLD IN IT: that's what's wanted. Snap the clasp open and the sun lights up distant peaks. Mechanical armies execute their maneuvers with the precision of a Swiss watch. The seasons rotate in close rhythm. An infinitely wide scope in an infinitely narrow compass: the most attractive quality of the book is that it can be held. The fifth-century poet T'ao Ch'ien buried himself in the countryside, escaping from the burdens of politics and bureaucratic infighting, and in his isolation he recovered the world in the form of a book, the *Book of Hills and Seas*:

> I have done my ploughing:
> I have sown my seed.
> Again I have time to sit and read my books . . .
> A gentle rain comes stealing up from the east
> And a sweet wind bears it company.
> My thoughts float idly over the story of King Chou.
> My eyes wander over the pictures of Hills and Seas.
> At a single glance I survey the whole Universe.
> He will never be happy whom such pleasures fail to please!

A Meditation on Reading

The old man whom I know only from a book – his own book, the one in which he invented himself and his isolated farm, his wine, his books – finds in his book something large enough to encompass myself reading over his shoulder: I am read.

The book is so small that your hand closes over it. The stanza that encapsulates the City of the World has been printed in tiny letters. The book is a miniature version of another book, just as that book was a miniature version of the world. How small can it get? You get down to the synopsis of a synopsis: where ten sentences stood for a hundred, here one sentence stands for those ten, a single sentence seeks to encompass the matter of the unfinishable and infinitely expansible encyclopedia. These are shells: the aphorism and the epic, the chanson de geste, the Grail story, the beast fable. The whole shape of each is implicit in its smallest band, the cusp is already the nave, the box contains nothing other than its own shape.

It all has to get smaller and smaller. That's the only hope of hanging on to anything at all.

Votive panels are crammed together, squeezing in as many saints and episodes as possible: The Great Discoverers, Famous Beauties of History, Stories from the Opera House, Little Tales from Plutarch. The reader needs a central postal box, a pool where all the names in the world come to be sounded and thereby made tangible and accessible: The Literary Guild! The Heritage Club! The Reader's Club! *Good Reading! Masterpieces of World Literature in Digest Form! The Story of the World's Literature,* illustrated with somber woodcuts of Callimachus! Virgil! Isaiah! Walther von der Vogelweide! François Villon! Victor Hugo! Alessandro Manzoni! An unending hall of portraits lit only by the immeasurably deep and prophetic eyes of the immortals! Four-page plot summaries of five-hundred-page novels extracting a final perfume from the vanishing pages of *Hypatia; Trilby; The Deemster; Peg Woffington; John Halifax, Gentleman; The Wreck of the Grosvenor; The Abbé Constantine; The Last of the Barons*!

It's a victory over time to shrink all the hours that would have been spent reading them into these minutes in which I scan sea voyages and ecclesiastical careers, feudal conspiracies and backstage intrigues. I speed up time, the element of which the storyteller is master, with his retards and accelerations, his surprises and crescendoes. I have cheated him. Sneaking up from behind, I purloin his secret list of resolutions to all stories, the taxonomy of climaxes, the little treatise on the arts of distraction and complication. I tear open the box of stories looking for what was still hidden in it, the one I haven't heard.

The Book That Read Itself

IMAGINE READING such a condensation and finding it to be the story of someone reading a particular book for the first time. The plot, such as it is, amounts to nothing more than this reader's encounter with a putatively extraordinary book, an encounter that precipitates an unpredictable and overwhelming sequence of events, events that transform him, yet so removed from ordinary experience that even I, the reader of the book – the only other person privileged to know of them at all – can just barely guess their real import. Imagine reading on, in the blissful assurance that this book (the book, that is, about the reader reading the book) will be quite different from any other – that just as the book within the book will transform the fictitious reader, I too will be transformed by eavesdropping on the process.

Where would such a book have come from?

Perhaps he has been aware of the book for most of his life but unaccountably never opened it until now. It sat on a shelf but was too high to reach. Or he had been strictly warned against touching it, or was barred from it by a lock.

Or a dead uncle left it to him, the rover he never met, of whom dubious malefactions were rumored in Shanghai and Surinam. Or nobody knew it was there. It had fallen behind a heavy bureau not moved for a century or more. Or it might be a lost journal he's reading – something found under the floorboards of an abandoned house – or a sheaf of uncompleted poems marked over with successive layers of tentative corrections. It had been built into the wall. The house was a Chinese box constructed for the sole purpose of concealing the book within itself.

Or it just turns up on a shelf, in plain view, an object of no apparent value. It's the work of a child in another century. She was a deacon's daughter, brought up among Tacitus and law books (for her these were nature, just as much as the limestone deposits and mountain rills among which her father's house nestled), a prophetic invalid trapped in time. Interlarded among the prose fragments are a few personal documents, the certificate of a birth or a funeral, a picture in a locket, a doctor's prescription, a strand of hair, a letter of condolence. The occasional water stains might conceivably be the mark of tears, but there is no way of telling if they are the writer's or another's. It's possible that no one has ever read this work other than the person who wrote it.

There is a world in which she is trapped, a world reducible to nothing more than a vocabulary. What is she, more than the sum of sundial and butterfly, turnpike and compass and dusk, thundershower and private concert and fever, cathedral and tea, daisy and lapdog, Venus and July, waterspout, goldfinch, barometer, chimney smoke? Chalk, bog, herb, moth? Token, temper, persuasion, respect, delight? She makes a record of her days and they are all the same. She goes for walks, for as long as she can walk. She is propped up in a chair in a garden. When the garden grows too cold, she leans against pillows in her room and is able to look down into the garden. On rare occasions she listens to music. Newspapers and letters are read aloud among the family. The visitors whose appearances and disappearances she carefully notes nevertheless remain remarkably shadowy. "Mister Robertson stayed for a while in the afternoon." These intrusions impinge but do not touch anything essential in the conversations she holds with herself in this notebook. Evidently she wishes not so much to describe as to dissolve them.

She dissolves the visitors in words, just as she dissolves the light and the chill and the encroaching murmur of mortality. The words are ready to hand, in the books that line her father's shelves, books of sermons and political economy, books of ocean voyages and military campaigns, of thorny metaphysical speculation and of amorous canzonet and hearty drinking song. Here she begins to compile her countervocabulary, her secret word list corresponding to meanings of her own private designation.

Some days she likes best the words in the moldiest of the books, the words used to describe the deaths of Protestant martyrs, the varieties of sin by which the souls of the deceased are encumbered, the hierarchical layers of etiquette accruing to the lower orders of the nobility. She develops an infinitely patient attitude toward the driest and stingiest of these words, those that seem to withhold any meaning but the most defensive and limiting.

She cultivates ancient pedantries and makes a garden out of them. Like a child performing in home theatricals, she assumes the voice of a dry old man, the solitary resident of an attic room within whose precincts he reaches judicious conclusions about the state of things. It is play to her, stroking her imaginary beard and murmuring aphorisms she invents on the spot, but the play wouldn't be fun if the pretend wisdom didn't fill her with real awe. When she takes on his voice it becomes possible to see beyond herself, to sketch the patterns of cities she will never visit and to envisage the outcome of battles not yet fought. She feels she flies.

As long as she writes, she inhabits an imitation of philosophy, such an imitation as could only be made by someone indifferent to philosophical rules. How much pleasure she must have had idling away the otherwise bland or painful days with her *Theory of Perception as a Process of Translation,* her *Treatise on Parallel Worlds,* her *Discovery of the Nervous Origin of Names.* All of these became part of her *Book of Explanations.* It wasn't written for anyone to read, even herself; it was written for someone to *write.* He could surmise the silly enjoyment she had taken in the forging of these solemnities, these make-believe doctrines, this claptrap of abstractions and numbered theorems. She had invented terms designed to clarify thoughts that had never been thought in the first place – what fun!

Threading his path among the journal entries, the secret reader feels her feeling her own way toward the century in which he in his turn is trapped. She writes her way out of an intolerable situation, as if the words were her future. She addresses him directly: To the Reader of the Future.

That phrase turns out to be the title of a lengthy and elaborate ode describing her vision of a world pervaded by what she calls Spirit, an "aetheric or incorporeal medium" under whose influence whatever in her day has been occulted or obscure will become bright and legible. In what she calls her "legend of anticipation," she goes so far as to wonder what this faceless future reader will make of her own poor words, whether he will be able to descry in them the fevers and unattainable longings that have racked her in what she describes as "my contemporary prison."

He begins to entertain the fiction that it is indeed himself and no other that she addresses. The words have been put in safekeeping so that he might redeem them. He begins to recognize the peculiar aspects of her writings, although he is aware that to another reader they might seem hard to distinguish from any amount of second-level work of the period in which she wrote, aware that their personae (the sky that figures as a character in her uncompleted verse drama, the leaves that acquire voices and speak in alternating strophes of their green youth, ruddy maturity, and sere decay) could easily be taken as the vaguest, the most ready-to-hand of symbols. Perhaps no one else will ever be able to discern in this manuscript what he has found there: a unique and specific correspondence, a chance conjunction of reader and book.

By the time he gets to the end, the book he reads becomes the book he might have written, as if the girl and her journal and her slow dissolution were his own invention. Or as if the book, which she did not complete but whose completed form he surmises, is identical to one that he imagined but did not write; he recognizes, with something like a shudder, the inner texture of his thoughts, the hidden moments of his life.

It's all in the accents, the pauses, the apparently inadvertent repetitions, the invisible shuffling between the turns of phrase. Her prose is a description of what it feels like to turn one's head and be taken unawares by something happening in the next room, an intimate mapping of how thoughts cope with being interrupted. She foresaw what he would be like. Her writing was a species of science fiction, an exercise in precognition in which she comprehended perfectly the way his mind would respond – a century and a half after her death – to her anticipatory description of that response.

In what space does he exist, if not inside her head, a head that exists nowhere but in his deciphering of her words? Or in her very hand as it traces the words on paper, the delicate muscles flexing and re-flexing as if in those movements they created meaning? The muscles of his own hand tingle in recognition. The dovetailing is so uncanny that he can only conclude that she has imagined him, that out of the depths of her imprisonment she has conjured up the ideal reader of her unfinishable book.

It is remotely possible that one of these condensations, one of these famous novels in digest form, contains the description of such a book, possible even that I have already read it, that I absorbed it at an early age, forgot it, and will someday be startled by a face-to-face encounter with a primevally early memory of its contents.

In that fashion I may one day share the fate of the Rhode Island professor of economics in H. P. Lovecraft's novel *The Shadow Out of Time,* who suddenly and inexplicably fell into a coma for five years and then, as suddenly, woke up with no memory of the intervening period. He was troubled afterward by nightmares of immense unearthly creatures inhabiting vast windowless libraries in which, for no apparent reason, he wrote out an account of his life and times. One day he received word that an expedition in the Australian desert had excavated the remains of an unknown civilization long predating human life on earth. He traveled to the site, and amid those ruins found a book, and with a gathering sense of fatality and horror ventured to open it:

> No eye had seen, no hand had touched that book since the advent of man to this planet. And yet, when I flashed my torch upon it in that frightful abyss, I saw that the queerly pigmented letters on the brittle, aeon-browned cellulose pages were not indeed any nameless hieroglyphs of earth's youth. They were, instead, the letters of our familiar alphabet, spelling out the words of the English language in my own handwriting.

The Browser's Ecstasy

As I crouch among these heaps of books – awkwardly, since at any moment a tower of delicately balanced volumes might fall on me or crash beyond easy retrieval – my hands and eyes move among pages encountered at random. In a few moments I will have seized on words from a dozen different books. They come upon me like the patches of hieroglyphs in a tomb revealed by the swaying of an archaeologist's lamp.

The rhythm is alternately staccato and oceanic, a succession of bee stings or a calm breeze from an unseen shore. By turns I'm lost, I seek, I find, I drop the thread again. Voices bark out phrases, then slam as quickly into silence. Maps are delineated in air. Lines of connection link up dissimilar objects and then break off. Meanings crawl around and then abruptly scatter like insects caught in a flashlight's beam.

What I am engaged in calls ideally for the juxtaposition of many books: the jumbled innards of a cupboard, the accumulations of a basement or an attic or a crammed shop filthy with age. Only by switching without interruption and as rapidly as possible can I appreciate the space dividing one book from the next and with any luck catch a glimpse of the potentially infinite lines connecting them.

I eavesdrop on the murmur of overlapping conversations. It's almost as if the books read each other, the way characters in novels read novels. I merely stand among them and read over their shoulders as characters in Raymond Chandler novels read Proust and Hemingway, characters in Henry James novels read novels by Paul Bourget, certain characters in Dostoevsky read the Bible while other characters in Dostoevsky read Bakunin, characters in Jane Austen read Mrs. Radcliffe, Don Quixote reads *Amadís de Gaula,* characters in *The Tale of Genji* read poems written by other characters in *The Tale of Genji,* characters in Dante spend an eternity in Hell remembering a book they read once.

But however absorbing it might be to get lost in the crisscrossing threads, it is the gaps, the blind pockets, the abrupt curtailments that are most bracing. Step into the hole and you've landed in a shuttered chamber, a snug dead end of the labyrinth. Nothing exists but the arbitrary contents of a stranger's hotel room: a razor, a ticket stub, a crumpled half-finished letter. The known universe is reduced to the dimensions of a detective novel by Freeman Wills Crofts.

A Meditation on Reading

INSPECTOR FRENCH WONDERS if his life has been a mistake. Inspector French eats a biscuit on the terrace of a Luxembourg hotel. Inspector French imagines his wife reading his written description of a river. Inspector French makes a checklist of clues: smears, abrasions, faulty registrations. Inspector French pauses to inhale the foreign air, crisp and invigorating. Inspector French decides to walk to the prefecture of police. Inspector French thinks about the warm, weathered tonality of the paving and facades of the small city. Inspector French is troubled by a recurring hesitation about a minor detail of the case – "The visitor put his hat down and then, a few moments later, with no evident motive, picked it up again" – a hesitation that prevents him from classifying it as routine. Inspector French wonders how long it will take for his letter to reach England. Inspector French visualizes the expression on the face of the man he interviewed earlier that day. Inspector French tries to recall if there is an adjective in the French language that would describe such an expression, and if so what its English counterpart would be. Inspector French admires the bustling energy of the marketplace in the center of town and compares it to similar scenes in London and other English cities. Inspector French feels the beginning of an unjustifiable elation, as if he had already "taped" a puzzle of which he has as yet, so far as he knows, not even the shadow of a solution.

Or turn the page and it's Canada, except it's better than

Canada. What a world to have plunged into, a world consisting of nothing but Canada! The great frozen river! The towering cliffs! The knives for trading! The account books! The wounds and amputations! The lathes and cobblestones! The tracts, the pamphlets, the petitions! The rough bearded woodsmen! The squaws grinding leather with their teeth! The canoes! The candles! The rats running up and down the ship cables! The owls! The impenetrable forest! The muskets! The boots! The embers! The strips of venison! The snow falling on top of snow! The trunks packed with tools and dry goods! The cabinets! The long tables! The shiny buttons on the military coats! The bayonets! The carts! The mist obscuring the harbor! The stray dogs! The locks, the bolts! The floorboards! The stone ramparts! The smoke rising from tiny islands in the middle of the river! The songs! The curses! The gurgles! The clusters of trees! The empty sky suddenly full of clouds! The voices swallowed up by the silence of the open sea!

A moment later it's a corridor in the hidden middle of the paranoid century, the reader's own. The central committee is on the verge of changing its opinion and a veteran opinion-monger prepares to find himself transformed into a demonic conspirator. Cigarette smoke in the corridor: the last trace the world will ever present for him. He feels himself metamorphosing into an idea, into an abstract noun. He *is* deviance, he *is* error. Before the bullet hits, he must make the transition and altogether *become* the word – as if it would hurt less to die as a noun than as flesh. As simple and neutral as being erased. He wants to feel almost as lucky as the cigarette smoke, whose spiraling evolutions are as close as he will ever again come to the contemplation of birds in flight.

Birds in flight pass over the urban garden where four tenants – apprentices who will one day be professionals – exchange identities several times over. They give parties where they pretend to be one another. In the shadows of a barbecue, one of them makes love with the reflection of another's companion. Hours later, the game of Scrabble is still going on, the triple word scores piling up with murderous intensity. Somebody will get lost on Second Avenue before the night is done. Somebody else will contemplate death in the night mirror, while on the blindly rotating turntable the Stravinsky clarinet music starts up for the third time.

Here, a child grew up to conceive of the past as a gallery of preserved glances: the weathered gaze across the top of wash bucket or tanning shed, the head turning from behind the plough, the boy running along the slope and waving his hands wildly in a form of sign language, the mute and almost unreadable nods half buried in smoke in a circle of elders. He remembers the origin of every gesture that has become habitual, the folk legend attached to every household chore. If he closes his eyes, the stones and bushes talk to him about everything they have witnessed. When he opens them again he notices that he has become his father.

There, a sophisticated woman in her middle years undergoes psychoanalysis and cabaret music. A sensitive dockworker loses control of his memory toward dawn in the Harlem side street where moments later an alcoholic novelist encounters him and they establish a surreal camaraderie. There are abortions and suicides. A chorus girl snorts cocaine while waiting for her industrialist boyfriend to show up. Gangsters play checkers in an anteroom. Foghorns echo down the river and the fuzzy shapes of barges create an effect like a modern painting. Strikes are ruthlessly suppressed by private security guards. Marriages end in laceration and broken glass. The city is decked for festival in bunting and brass bands. Old men dredge up fragments of battle scenes in basement-level taverns. A cracked record repeats the same mawkish phrase again and again. The Jersey shore disappears under a cloud of smoke from the ferry.

And there again, when I was a student at Heidelberg, I met a thin-lipped young man, we were feverish about metaphysics, and I fell in love with his sister and fought a duel with his father. Under the German bridge the German water ran over the German stones, a German willow tempered the harshness of the scene, while from an upper window a German woman shook out a rug. The houses in that country had peaked roofs like cowls and odd angular windows – *Erke,* they called them in their dialect – and, in the parlor of that house, which beyond all other houses I would come to know too well, were shadows from whose depths a crone seemed to emerge as if from a forest, only to be recognized an instant later as the woman who from the upper window had shaken the dust into the winding cobbled street. Somehow, crossing the space between parlor and garden, I could think of only three things: a handkerchief, a piano, and poison.

She sleeps on an island among ghosts. A red thread dangles from a tree and it is the entrance to the back of her church school, populated at night by cackling thieves and politicians' pimps. Letters in charcoal announce that the government has fallen, even when it hasn't. Mysterious fires are being set. Later she will learn that the dreaded arsonist is none other than her little friend, the clubfooted baker's boy, and she will surprise herself by blessing him for his misdeeds. But for now, crossing the space between vegetable plot and tourist bar, she can think of only three things: a spiderweb, a gemstone, and a knife for scaling fish.

Elsewhere, the bandits have set fire to the prairie. The Mormon police close in on the isolated homestead where the apostate has taken shelter. His daughter wants to teach a city slicker what life in the rough is all about, so that the slicker can help undo the crooked deal by which the deed to a mine was hidden in the mine itself. They learn to communicate by means of comparisons between different types of cloud formation: grandiose domes portending storm, sleek arrowlike dashes, lazy drooping hollows. She collapses and is taken to an undiscoverable cabin. He learns how to live without eating. They decide they can be comfortable in a place they will never leave.

Others had to learn how to live in apartments too small for beds, make money off vegetable rinds or strips of old newspaper, exist in cubicles defined by fumes and wheel grease. Opera was what escaped between the cracks in the colossal doors, an unattainable dream like Sunday or ocean. They struggled to become barbers, and lost. There was nothing left for them but the sound of somebody screaming a name, a name he had read once in a newspaper. The settlement was indifferent and filthy, at least that corner of it in which there were counters for selling used razors. People die without even being able to cancel their appointments.

Animals converse with the children of groundskeepers and instruct them in the hidden geography of large properties. Trees converse with other trees. Wars are fought over stores of nuts or the damming of millponds. In little paper boats they sail against the wilderness, making up rhymes about the grandfather of all squirrels and how he was robbed of his birthright. The earth is composed of bunks and stairways and gardens. Its inhabitants have played for so long at their extended game of hide and seek that some have no memory of ever being found.

You can also evade capture by being an exiled musician.

A Meditation on Reading

Register under a false name and count how many buses go by outside the hotel after midnight. The condition of freedom is to lack topics for conversation other than the discomfort of desire and the decay of the senses. You get bitter entertainment from contemplating the inauthenticity of each of your thoughts in succession. You spy on the machines in the bar. You line up against the wall. It is like inhabiting the paradise of the ersatz in the company of pensioners nostalgic for the acrid tobacco substitutes that were loosely packed into cigarettes during the Stalin era. The operator almost remembers you, just as you come close to remembering what happened last night: was it a sailor that you beat up outside the fire station, or yourself that was beaten up by a sailor? The impasto of scraped names and maledictions on the wall in front of you serves as a sort of harbor.

The harbor freezes. It is a Baltic dynasty into whose foundering you have been admitted. A deranged nursemaid mutters prophecies about a lost twin returning from exile. Moments later she is stabbed by hired ruffians. Among astrolabes and reliquaries, a blind diplomat laments the crimes he has covered up over a lifetime. The outriders get drunk and sing ballads about the origin of the state. The hero would have gotten married if there hadn't been a civil war. During long intervals, courtiers circle around one another while harpsichord music plays, music imported all the way from Munich ("the very latest thing, I'm told"); there are long debates about political appointments; poison is administered. After the ice jam in the first chapter, you know already that in the last there will be a conflagration and that from its embers, somehow, a nation will be born.

Or, along a road afflicted with war wreckage and loan-sharking, you can trade trinkets for valuable clasps, negotiate with a serving maid, masquerade as a resurrector of dead benefactors. Hide from soldiers; follow the smell of burning meat; spy out the predilections of traveling companions; pass untouched through the aftermath of massacres. They even imitate wounds, pretend to be blind so they can pass signals to cardsharps. Yet none are more corrupt than those they gull. False prophecy, in the hands of clairvoyant beggars, is revealed as the most honest of professions.

Or you can find yourself dropped within the coordinates of an Alexandrian revel, to riot among couches yellow and silken, muttering into tawny hair the elements of a lexicon of pleasure: tongue, fire, curtain, clasp, haunch, damask, laugh, ring, belly, string, ivory, murmur, willow, droplet, gleam, tile, ripple, nibble, shriek, flute. In the perfumed bath the Ionian courtesan sang us a long song full of names and numbers, in which all the names rhymed amusingly with one another and every number was a different color.

By Stealth

I BROWSE. It gets darker. I continue to browse, I will continue to browse. I am being sustained by an activity difficult to describe and even more difficult to justify. The constant shifting of attention from one object to another is like a bird's way of looking, cocking the neck from side to side to scan the visual field for signs of edible life. Life teems everywhere in these parts. The books are made of the stuff. Poke the beak in – turn up a wriggling mass of syntax, pick out a few juicy nouns, the swelling curve of an assertion – yank away from that rock toward the next – repeat the process a dozen times – shift uphill a bit and start again with a fresh batch.

Proper reading, reading in a straight line, is something else again. That is a task, with its procedures, regulations, orders. The reader wants to get at something and in turn is gotten at. The mechanism cannot function unless he lays himself open at the precise angle and aligns his head with the slot marks. There are foreseeable consequences. He's going somewhere and at the end of the journey there will be questions.

To move through a book from beginning to end is to advance triumphantly toward the death that waits after the last word of the last sentence. Each time out, it is a little rehearsal of dissolution. Assemble the pieces, see them through their matings and agons, and then share their disappearance. Of course, one can begin again, again and again. But still there is a desire for something else, an altogether different kind of movement. It's a sort of hermetic spiraling, no more static than the vibrant stillness of the hummingbird at the window. In short, browsing: the path that has no ends and no beginnings, where all is middle.

It is such luxuriance, a voluptuousness of sustained duration that allows time to come into its own and somehow step outside itself. To amble through a sentence as if it existed independently of any other sentence, to feel out its particular pockets and eddies, to allow its implicit rhythm to pervade all surrounding space. Isn't this as much as we're granted, this corner of nature at long last (as it was in the beginning) truly ours, the language we were born in and that fits us like a body? I get lost in the garden and forget what time it is, or what time is.

Browsing has the feel that the Japanese describe as *wabi,* translated in one dictionary as "quiet taste" but implying – or so I was told in a language instruction book I browsed in once – something old, worn smooth with use, simple, durable, made more beautiful by the passage of time. A stone ink bowl, slightly chipped but still good for at least a few more centuries. It's satisfying like an encounter in a country lane with an old gentleman with whom you are ever so slightly acquainted, the glint of whose eyes reaches you from under the brim of his hat just as the light fails. How well do you need to know him? You've already shared as much of his mind as you ever could even if you had a hundred years.

The book isn't single and solid; it's a permeated field, a pool. Impossible even to catch sight of all the elements swimming around in there. The patterns they make change constantly. From the transient impressions created by those patterns a ghost book is made, incorporeal and evanescent, unique to a particular reader. It hovers in the air a moment around my head: a book of glints and murmurs and profiles that I catch sight of, inhabit for an instant, and let slide. The light falls slantwise on a sentence isolated from its surroundings. Only once is it given to catch sight of that island, lost on every other occasion in a mist of words.

Disarranged and truncated, the vocabulary of an antiquated history (this time around it is *The Liberation of Italy* by Countess Evelyn Martinengo Cesaresco) regroups into oases of disjunctive detail: "He massed his troops at all the entrances to the city, so that at dawn he might strangle the insurrection by a concentric movement, as in a noose." "As he walked from his carriage to the stairs, an unknown individual pushed against him on the right side, and when he turned to see who it was, the assassin plunged a dagger in his throat." "He believed that his footsteps were dogged by three individuals, one of whom was an ex-French convict." "The silence of the Campagna was only broken by little gusts of a chilly wind off the Tiber; it seemed as if a spectral army moved without sound."

The sentences in the books I have read sequentially are nothing to the sentences come upon by stealth, raided in the middle of their stories. Tearing open the theologies of Byzantium or the memoirs of a pickpocket, I catch a glimpse of its heart and read the future there: even if it is only the future of my reading, the first inkling of a volume I will finally come to know so well that half a lifetime later the sentences will be furniture scuffed with long use, a surface marked endearingly with nicks and gashes and flaking varnish. I will by then have sat among the words so long that they will seem to bear the impress of my shape as much as I bear the impress of theirs.

Yet even after so many years I will find the unknown in the known, come upon a jarringly strange phrase in the most familiar text. In fact, it is precisely those familiar texts that are at heart most strange. Coming upon them obliquely, when they are not expecting me, I catch them at their strangeness, madly swirling fish that have not yet sensed the presence of the fisherman.

Virgil's Lot

BROWSING IS THE ATTEMPT to keep alive a last irrational remnant of the old world, the lost world of divination and magic signs. "Seek and ye shall find." I know I'm doing something a machine can't do. A machine cannot be so purposefully arbitrary, cannot close its eyes and make a wish at the same time. It cannot seek to get lost in this fashion, allowing itself to drop in confident free fall toward the heart of a wilderness. It cannot find what it has not been programmed to seize on.

Browsing is a faint tracing of an ancient discipline, the *sortes virgilianae* of the Roman seers. Open the *Aeneid* anywhere and you see the future, or the road that leads to the future. Perhaps, as with Charles I and Lord Falkland in the Bodleian library, it will provide bitter instruction, an invitation to your own overthrow.

Instead of the skin of slain sheep, those in search of prophecy can wrap themselves in the skin of the omen poem. Rather than search the vein lines in the livers of slaughtered animals, they can scan the occult patterns in "the freights of flitting ghosts" and "the margin of the fatal flood." Virgil, the conjure man, cunningly laid into his words all potential meanings, to be activated on contact with the properly attentive reader. These are the leaves in which time is wrapped, ready for unfolding.

Nor does it lie there inert. The future with which the book is alive stirs and turns. It moves around in the dark. The lines change places when no one is reading them. Perhaps they change places depending on who is reading them, so that no two people dip into the same book. The encounter of a particular reader and a particular line, at a particular point in time, is a reality without precedent or successor. The river does not repeat itself.

The line can come from anywhere. Perform the analogous act with the Bible, the *Aeneid*'s distinguished successor (or predecessor, depending on what direction you read it from), the scriptures that Virgil had already anticipated in the cryptic lines of the fourth Eclogue as if he were a privileged advance reader. But then, according to Tertullian, the Greek and Roman classics were themselves derived from the Hebrew Bible: "Who among the poets, who among the sophists, has not drunk from the fountain of the prophets? From them the philosophers have slaked their thirst of mind. . . . If they invented these things out of their own feelings, then our mysteries must be counted copies of what came later – a thing contrary to nature. For the shadow never exists before the body, nor the copy before the truth."

A Meditation on Reading

The point is moot in any event if the Bible had existed (as from a certain point of view it must have) all along in the mind of God, if indeed the Bible were not in some sense (as from a slightly different point of view it must have been) indistinguishable from the mind of God, without variance of priority or nature. If the world was latent in God from before time, then the world's books were there too – including, among all the others, the *Aeneid*. Go back to the source and you find everything waiting for you. The map tells you not only where you are going but where you came from.

It is a lost magic. The machine, merciless in its logic, cannot understand the function of divination and in consequence refuses to reconstitute it. Its reluctantly offered substitute is synthetic food cooked up in a lab. We find ourselves steeped in an aroma of the inhuman. Strictly authentic randomness, scientifically certifiable chance: that is what the machine offers, but not what we really wanted, even though we said that was what we wanted.

We wanted a chance in which will could somehow play a role, in which desire could magically skew the results, an oracle which without conscious intervention or cheating would impart a longed-for omen. The machine provides a randomness that is beyond our influence and therefore neither helpful nor interesting. Mechanically concocted chance has no savor, no reassuring smell of smoke signals or burnt offerings, no earthy odor of dried yarrow stalks.

PERHAPS INDEED THE LINE CANNOT come from just anywhere. Not just any accident will do. To believe that Virgil's lottery will yield a relevant truth, you must already feel that the source book, whether *Aeneid* or Bible, is so seamless a fabric that any shred of it holds wisdom whole. It's imbued in heal-all, in ultimate meaning. The stain runs too deep to be bleached out by time or weather or the fires set by marauders.

Or: the book is a box of threads that somewhere tie together, each of its lines literally a line one can clutch at to be hauled to safety. Such is the blind faith of the shipwrecked.

A Bible retrieved from a foundering ship brings light in darkness to Robinson Crusoe: "Only having opened the book casually, the first words that occurred to me were these, 'Call on me in the day of trouble, and I will deliver, and thou shalt glorify me.'" Likewise, a Bible cast up miraculously from the ocean solaced other castaways on Jules Verne's Mysterious Island. The computer's fragmentary statistic, by contrast, cannot even properly be called a fragment. It was never part of a whole. The reef its numbers are forming by blind accretion does not yet exist. A printout in a bottle would be cold comfort. What could it offer any castaway but an agonizing reminder of just how far he had fallen from any link to the mainland?

A Little Treatise on Ways of Reading

But isn't this, after all, heaven? This island of books where I am free to look at what I like, linger on what I like? I am in full control. The books exist to be played on by my faculties. They cannot evade me, nor can they hold me a moment longer than I want them to.

If the sentences knew how I had read them . . .

But there is nothing they can do. Freedom roves at will among the forms of pretending, as if they were a museum of masks and gestures. The reader can do what he likes here. There are styles of reading as there are styles of writing, as many as the reader can invent. Can I enumerate them? I compose a little treatise in my head, resting my eyes for a few moments from all this fine print, these ornamental chapter headings.

1. He can read by letting the eye rove over the shapes of the letters and find patterns in their textures and clusterings, the distinctive fur patterns and topographic markings, so that an extract of Herrick or Melville becomes — even before the eye can make

out the words — as recognizable by its grain as a patch of land seen from a helicopter.

2. He can read as if feasting, nourished by the words as by food and drink.

3. As if the words were part of his body, as if the inwardly sounded syllables literally coursed through him.

4. As if hearing a music not bound by time, in whose phrases he can abide as long as he likes; as if massaged internally by the syllables.

5. As if the text were just now coming into being and he were present at the moment of writing, of pen scratching against paper.

6. As if inside someone else's head, watching the intimate spectacle of that person's thinking, or as if he simply were that person and were now reading over what he had himself written.

7. As if the text were magical, and made unreal things appear and move; as if everything described in it were actually occurring at the moment of reading.

8. As if the words were alive.

9. As if in their natural state the words would have scattered an instant later, like sparrows or water striders, and it was only by chance that their momentary conjunction had been frozen as by a snapshot.

10. As if each word were alive and had a purpose; as if the words danced together in an elaborate and frantic choreography in order to enact a collective message, like cheerleaders or Red

A Meditation on Reading

Guards spelling out WE'RE NUMBER ONE or THE EAST IS RED; as if the shapes of stanzas and paragraphs evolved from arcane social rituals practiced by the words among themselves; as if by looking at how they grouped themselves on the page you could form some slight idea of what they were thinking. Or as if the text as a whole were a single conscious being, capable of "bristling" or "breathing" or "insinuating."

11. As if the words had literally been kept alive by human blood; as if they were the end product of a scientific experiment to prolong the human life span by unnatural means; as if this experiment had been conducted on the basis of a scientific theory that words possessed uncanny and unmentionable powers.

12. As if examining a patch of local foliage; as if the words had forced their way out of the earth; as if the text, once above ground, had aged and become overgrown with moss, had been bored into by insects, had grown thin and brittle. As if by gauging the maturity of the text, how far it had gotten from its origin, the reader measured his own span.

13. As if unintended patterns were revealed in scourings, weatherings, erosions.

14. As if the text were mute and communicated through a kind of dumb show.

15. As if the only significant elements were those left out.

The Age of Memory

IN THE QUIET OF THE BOOK depot I hear a low rumble, the sound of a disappearance occurring in slow motion. That the dislocations of that temblor are experienced in deceptively gentle increments doesn't make them any less destructive. Whole languages, whole systems of marriage and heraldry leak into the cracks. I need only stare at this heap long enough to glimpse the literal eating up of knowledge. Words are blotted out under the spread of foxing and mottling. I may be the last who will ever read this book.

Things get written down on notepaper and then thrown away. Books undergo a similar process, only slower. The words that speak of eternity are corroding moment by moment. Even if they survive a bit longer, they may live on in a world where the memory of how to read them has fallen into disuse, like those useless volumes among which the effete illiterate Eloi of *The Time Machine* held their mindless feasts.

It doesn't really come back, the thing that was written down. Tiny pieces of it come back, to fewer and fewer in each generation. At a certain point they stop caring; I stop caring. There are curates, and colonels, and even diarists about whom I have lost all curiosity, sermons and treatises on political economy good only for lining drawers. I don't have time for them. It is simply a matter of housekeeping, of maintaining as much empty space as comfort requires. Knowledge as clutter, to be swept out to let air and light in.

Everything will not disappear, only most aspects of everything. Some marks are bound to persist. We brush past archaic scratches, some of them disguised as the effects of cataclysmic weather. A millennium or two of conscious existence might find itself – in the ultimate condensation, the most laconic of masterpieces in digest form – reduced to a few cryptic grooves on a cairn. Which scratch will stand for you, or you, ten thousand years hence? In how many centuries does an emotional pattern become a geological formation?

THERE WAS A TIME BEFORE BOOKS and there will be, even if I cannot imagine it, a time after books. I stand at a moment in a historical trajectory. A certain quantity of knowledge has been gathered into these books, or has clung to them almost by accident; there have been earlier gatherings, earlier dispersals; a further and quite likely more radical dispersal will follow. Once again, as at Alexandria and Constantinople, Ch'ang-an and Baghdad, the laboriously collected facts will be broken up and burned.

Later, facts will be gathered again, but they will not be the same facts, or even the same kinds of facts. But the gatherers will not know that. They will reinvent the lore of my world as I reinvent the mind of an inhabitant of Afrodisias or of the kingdom of the Lombards. They will enjoy themselves by making everything up and calling it knowledge.

Learning was more obviously malleable in the time of the walking book, when the death of a griot was like a library burning. In such a world, knowledge exists when it is present. It consists of what can be called up from memory at a given moment, and waxes and wanes with age and health and circumstance. Wisdom is a person who walks into the room and sits down. Each recital is absolute. There was never a certifiable recital before; there may never be another. In the kingdom of rumor, the auditors will remember they heard it but they'll never be able to prove what exactly it was about. It had doors in it; layers of gates; a succession of tricks, of question-and-answer games; catalogues of birds and conjurors; the fall of a city; the celebration of a wedding and its destructive sequel, that sudden violent incursion.

More likely they will remember being impressed by the strength of the reciter's memory. It was a feat apt for heroes, but you had to be there. He sang the whole thing from beginning to end and never made a mistake. Wish I could hear it again. They don't make memories like that anymore. The old people remembered twice as much. The people before the old people remembered absolutely everything, like God or like the ill-fated Funes the Memorious of Borges, for whom the fall of each leaf became an indelible, inescapable imprint.

In the latter days of recitation, memory became a frail thing. It needed props, mnemonic numbering devices: rhymes and meters, three wishes and seven brothers, systematic catalogues of ships and dynasties, the repertoire of standard fill-ins and formulae. Without a book to look anything up in you had to sweat every detail, thankful for any trick that would help shore it up, so that when the cue came around you wouldn't flounder. Hence there are limits to the repertoire. There will not be an infinite number of ballads, although there may well be an extravagant number of verses and a virtually infinite number of ways to combine them. Knowledge is limited to what a human can carry around with him. World without storage, without indexes, where the sage figures as animate spinal encyclopedia and the acolyte spends ten years in training, learning how to become a book.

A thousand years go by, two thousand years, and the Veda or the Zuni prayer remains intact. The universe has been kept in order by sheer force of memory, a force redoubled by terror at the unimaginable consequences of getting it wrong. A single syllable out of place can rip the invisible fabric and wreck the balance of the cardinal points. By this curious portage they have wrapped meanings in sounds and carried the sounds in their bodies across potentially infinite stretches of time. The text – a live thing, slippery and quivering – is maintained without interruption in their living bodies. Death never touches it.

The Coming of the Book

How did this thing start, this domino effect of scribbles eliciting further scribbles? Why write anything down? Because they got tired of carrying it and because they couldn't afford to drop it. The lists got longer, the consequences of error more dire. It was a massive shifting of weight, shuffling off a burden never really noticed until it wasn't there anymore. A labor-saving device freeing memory from the obligation to replay everything that ever happened once every day, so as not to run the risk of a crucial item slipping into the inaccessible.

Not entertainment or even the sacred provided the most pressing occasion for writing things down, but a simple overload of the enumerating faculty. More things were happening and they were happening faster. Never so many cattle or captives in living memory. Hence the oldest forms of written literature: roll call, order of battle, slave roster, inventory, bill of lading, itemized receipt. Wanted: data entry cuneiformist, good wedge technique, 50 wpm or better.

Only much later, perhaps during the post-harvest

downturn, did the scribes get around to making a permanent record of things that had already been committed to memory by specialists, as a sort of backup file. It must have been something of an afterthought, the idea that you could fit the whole sacred epic on twenty tablets. Certainly it provided employment for the scribes, an opportunity to keep their skills fresh while waiting for the next slave haul.

But once that incredible job of transcription had been completed – how many lines did they fill in any which way because there was no one on hand just at that moment who could recall the way it went? – once the tablets had been trimmed and baked and formally presented, how often would anyone actually drag them out to read? Was it simply a nice feeling to know that they were there, duly archived? And how long would it have taken to realize that not actually needing to memorize them had taken off the edge, that the ability to reel off the whole *Enuma Elish* without looking at the script was ineluctably reduced from sacred task to mere stunt?

They must have noticed, if only for a moment, how strange transcription made the sacred epic look – or rather how strange was the fact that it "looked" like anything. Up until then, it wasn't an object. It had no body except for the bodies it seized on to perpetuate itself, the bodies of the memorizers. If the text had any kind of physical reality, it included the smells in the room where it was recited, the shifts of light and temperature, the breath of the listeners. Written down, its familiar pronouncements became curiously neutral shapes, just so much furniture. The experience was alienating, like hearing your voice played back on a tape recorder, especially if you have never encountered a tape recorder before. The poem that included the universe, that had in some sense given birth to the universe, was contained in a chunk of clay you could hold in your hand.

The poem itself changed. What made perfect sense when the reciter performed it seemed weirdly transformed when translated into letters. The eye found gaps imperceptible to the ear. Contradictions in chronology that no one had ever noticed became glaring when two tablets were placed side by side. As if all that time – some thousand years or so – they hadn't really grasped what it was about, hadn't ever quite gotten the whole picture of the narrative: they had lived in the suspended instants of each turn in the story. When it was being read aloud, everything that lay in store was mysterious, unattainable until its moment of emergence came. Now it was possible to sneak a peek at the next tablet, jump to the end of the adventure. As a result, they looked at it more coldly, laid out as on a military map, something they had made theirs. Resonances capable of bridging the distance between earth and sky were subdued and imprisoned in a cage of wedge marks.

The scribe pressing the wedge down – savoring the

clean cut in wet clay – saw that by the casual rearrangement or omission of one or another letter the sense of the universe could be altered. He could hardly help but realize how drastically he could distort a text simply by letting his hand slip, whether he regarded that possibility with dread or amusement. Dread at first no doubt, but after the five hundredth clay tablet a bit of amusement must have begun to creep in, all the more intense for being absolutely barred from expression. There are no jokes like the ones you can get killed for telling. (Was it somebody's idea of a joke that a Bible published in 1631 – the so-called Wicked Bible – printed the Seventh Commandment as "Thou shalt commit adultery"?)

IN THE TRANSCRIBING, and in the reading over of the transcription, the arbitrariness of the text becomes fatally apparent even if unacknowledged. It was born arbitrary, that first text to which all others are footnotes, appendices, sequels, rewrites. Later came system, continuity, cause and effect, story logic, world-historical schemata. What went down first came out of nowhere, and it shows.

The first chapters in the book are the ones that make everybody crazy, permanently, because they can never be explained. They are a mixed bag of mismatched sentences tied to nothing, surrounded by the blankness of what from now on (once the fleeting opportunity went by four thousand years ago) can never be written down. The first sentences mean everything because they have to bear the full weight of the silence they break. If nothing else survived, nothing else exists. Here is all the origin we will ever have.

The people of the book are held captive by what cannot be crossed out. This will always be the way the story starts. The book is history, in so intolerable and viselike a fashion that the book must be converted into escape from history. The way out is the way in. From the very words of the book I make different words. Scriptures are the most spacious of books, furnished with the roomiest gullies.

Every item that a word can name is more than itself, placed there as a sign, a reminder of something previous which is not yet – by this token, this fig or string or bed or rib – lost beyond recovery. By such small increments, a word at a time, I return, under the camouflage of knowledge and indeed in the very heart of the repository of knowledge, to that paradise of unknowing in which words were inseparable from what they stood for. I go to the book to be delivered from what the book means. In the outrageous freedom of that place, the bushes of speech simply sprang forth. The earth shook and trembled without any awareness on my part that a given sentence – a sentence such as "the earth shook and trembled" – had been written by a person or had an ulterior purpose beyond its own shaking and trembling. In those fields – I mean the sentences – a force was manifest, as rough as what thrust the outer layers aside to let the blossom out.

Sacred story, here, meant that story itself was sacred. What matter what it told? It was enough to say "it was."

The secret reader creeps in when the words aren't paying attention. It had better be in secret, because he has come to look at things under a different light, to see how the stories behave after the supervisors have locked up for the night. As if watching water dash against rock, lost in the violent flow of pattern-making, he sees the episodes play out: the one about the children in the fiery furnace, the handwriting on the wall, the pillar of salt, the rod turned into a serpent, the angels stopping by for a drink disguised as humans, the boy with the father's blade poised to slash his throat, the enemy tribes pelting or being pelted with stones, the prophet blinded and bound, the head on the plate, the head held up bleeding, the youth hung by his hair, the kingdom divided, the witch in the cave, the emperor walking on all fours and eating grass, the sky turning black at midday, the dream foretelling famine, the boy sold into slavery by his brothers, the boy playing the harp, the woman cast out into the desert, the ladder rising into the sky, the basket set adrift, the man pretending that his wife is his sister, the smooth-skinned brother and the hairy brother, the fair sister and the dark sister, the queen fed to the dogs, the ass breaking into speech, the sky raining nourishment, water gushing from the rock, the prophet thrown in prison, the son conspiring against his father, the hero staring down from his rooftop at the young woman in her bath, the hero sending her husband to his death, the wise man condemned to the darkness of his royal solitude, the wise man gnawing on darkness, the wise man eaten by crows, the wise man riding toward the clouds in his chariot.

The story is a drill that keeps digging. No matter what stage it's at (he sees her, he sends for her, he's giving the command about her husband, he's being rebuked by the old man), it's always the instant of breakthrough. The crust cracks, the word speaks. Whatever episode I scan is happening now – the elders at this moment are plotting to entrap the virtuous girl, the brothers are just on the verge of betraying the youngest among them – just like the previous ones and just like those yet to come. The book is superior to the reader because it's simultaneously alive in all its parts, not only those that the reader, with his limited capacity for attention, can focus on at any given moment.

The Middle of the Thing

Each sentence is bent out of shape by the sentences that came before, as if a pin mangled on a conveyor belt deformed each widget in turn, and each twisted widget wrought further damage as it rolled along. Each sentence wants to move backward, not from nostalgia but in a doomed attempt to rewrite its ancestors, to restrain them from passing sentence. It wants to be the first sentence, to lay down from scratch its own grammar, its own vocabulary. It's horrible to emerge so late in the story, with most of the plot already worked out and the options of the characters drastically circumscribed by what happened earlier.

The sequence of the sentences cannot be undone, nor the events they inscribe. No way to go back and erase or revise the earlier chapters. Every step was necessary, even the curiously redundant or ineffectual ones. To read the book is to contemplate a tortuous irrevocability.

Sequence, in its rudimentary phase, was the laying of fragments side by side. Call them rock one, rock two, rock three. Later a suspicion might dawn that rock three came before rock two, but by then it's too late to reverse a sequence that has become the basis for every subsequent assertion. Whatever else might have been legible has become part of the dark counterhistory of the erased, the unspeakable chronicle of how names came into being, how the inventors of words were dismembered and their memory eradicated, how the destroyers renamed every object and established a perimeter within which words could be spoken as if they had just been dreamt up.

The epic starts in the middle of the thing because that is where it finds itself. It has to figure out how it got there. It builds the door by which it will eventually discover itself to have entered: the inlet, the burning palace, the deserted oasis. The story comes into being at a vantage point from which it can begin to discern the shape of the path already traveled, the itinerary of a forgotten night journey whose vistas and rest stops must be handmade piece by piece to provide the hero with a memory. He had an oar, and therefore had traveled by water; consequently there must once have been a far shore.

Any book reaches back to earlier books, the books it answers or quotes from or imitates or steals from, books that in turn refer back to yet earlier models. Every script is a patchwork daubed together from what already exists. The chain recedes until you reach the source that can only be imagined, the well of lost speech, the point of origin that is also a point of rupture. Pausing at the rim of that black tunnel – the spot that might be marked with the inscription "Here everything else vanished" – I gain unaccountable energy from the contemplation of what is irrecoverably blotted out.

Having run down the scale, I run it back again, riffing from past to present and then back, to end again at the beginning, when the book was not yet opened, the story not yet begun. It becomes a habitual pastime, a small-scale rehearsal of death and birth. The flourishing and decadence of immense traditions become chapters in a chapbook, a chaplet, a rosary of cataclysms. Even the idea of oblivion reassures as long as there is a name for it.

But where did being come into being if there was no place already set up for it? What language did it think in, if there wasn't any language yet? The point of origin is also the limit of what it is permissible to imagine.

A Genealogy

He reads the inherited record as a child of nine or ten – confident of his own newfound maturity – will survey his old handwritten papers and perceive them as the work of a succession of almost incomprehensible beings who have disappeared, leaving behind only these scrawls.

With the child's accession to reading and writing, an infantile ecosphere of labyrinthine intrigue and elastic metaphor was irretrievably lost. Whole systems of correspondence, fluidities of identity, interlocking mazes of linked meaning, went under. It had to do with an inability to keep up. Even if brain could still think that fast, hand could not record nor eye decipher with sufficient speed; and by now it seemed that what could in no way be recounted or recorded could not be said truly to exist. The age of writing was in consequence an age of gross simplification.

A straightening out of neuronal tangles, a reduction of possibilities to as many lines as even the quickest scribe could handle, and only a child just arrived in the country of literacy would have enough recollection of the territory left behind to ask, Is that supposed to show what thinking is like? That simplistic and arbitrary patch of blots?

No, just some marks as reminders. Bone scratches, powder smears. To extrapolate from them, you really had to have been there. The child can at a certain point remember precisely what the scribble represented, however verbally undefinable that object or location might be. Not long afterward, he no longer remembers but – so to speak – remembers having remembered.

The old scrawls are discarded shells, a midden of identities. The primeval forebear is the root infant, first to leave a surviving mark, inscrutable originator whose imperious chaos disdains even the suggestion of form, mythological dynastic founder for whom wall or any available surface was a sky on which he sketched in broad sweeps the known universe.

Afterward came the builders of alphabets with their reversed letters and upside-down names, themselves succeeded by ever more finicky generations of clerks and pedants who took petty pride in their ability to restrain the impetuous lines, to rein in the loops and tie them securely to the mast, to suppress the vowels' impulse to puff up and sprawl half across the page, until, in the final and most legalistic age, exaggerated care is taken that the dots and crossbars are in their proper positions, every line straight, the end of every sentence marked with a full stop.

A Meditation on Reading

Here the most archaic is the most infantile, and the most mature is the most recent descendent. By reversing the process, by scraping away accumulated barnacles of vocabulary and allusion, the reader might hope to regress to a lost paradise of pervasive babble. There plays teasingly along the brink of recollection the syntax of an untutored and unrestrained tongue that could (without intending anything of the kind) articulate groves and cloudbanks, engender a glossolalia of celestial rivalries and gropings, cosmic histories written in saliva and mud, like the worlds sung effortlessly into being by the subarctic magicians of the Finnish *Kalevala* (itself a work retrieved from folk memory at the last possible hour, written down in the nineteenth century when the chain of oral transmission was beginning to weaken).

But they have gone away, the old magicians, to the other side of memory. They continue to live there in ingeniously concealed caves and hollows. Once in a while they choose to pay an impromptu visit, seeking only an appropriate spot to alight. Where? They have found it. The tip of the tongue: and are gone.

Archives

A FURTHER UNINTENDED CONSEQUENCE of writing language down was to make it numerical. A visible object occupying space is measurable. What is transcribed into characters and lines can be counted. The means by which the book would disappear was latent in the first sentence of the first book. A future digitalization was implicit in the initial contact of reed incisor with soft clay. Here was planted (precisely in the manner of one of their almost formless deities blindly and violently futtering the universe into shape) the seed of the quantified word, the electronic kabbalah, the sefirot of networks.

The word finally, as if it were unalterable destiny, becomes electronic. To reduce speech to a pattern of numbers makes it absolute as mathematics, eternally durable like relations between numbers. A full set of instructions for replicating a small library can be encoded in a single chip: this is supposed to be a way of saving the word, stabilizing it for purposes of preservation. The rotting heap before me is dying and can be kept alive only, in the manner of a science fiction story, by being converted into another form of matter.

In practice, however, computerization marks the return of language to primordial fluidity. Digitalized writing is unavoidably about erasure. It's analogous to the progression from letters that people preserve (wrapped in ribbon and tucked in a box in a dry place) to telephone conversations that evaporate as they occur, so that the twentieth century became the era of irretrievable dialogue, whole lives leaking into the ether without leaving a mark.

As the word dematerializes, it becomes easier to dispose of. The archive of clay will outlast the archive of bytes. Assuming, that is, that the will to preserve even exists. Miniaturize all the information, gather it in a central corral: it sounds like the ideal setup for a wipeout. What wouldn't world-class book-burners like Shih Huang-ti or Bishop Ambrose have given for a device able to expunge all philosophy and heresy from human memory with a single keystroke, like that single neck that Caligula wished on the people of Rome so that he might decapitate all of them at once?

And so the day arrives when the book is seen as an unnecessarily permanent way to record information, imposing the ghostly presence of out-of-date thoughts by sheer material bulk. The books drive out the present in the same way that piles of old newspapers eat up a room's space. The volumes of the useless encyclopedia remain locked forever in 1932. In an ideal world it might be interesting to preserve them, but they take up needed space. Their mere persistence costs money. Only reasonable that people should begin to ask what is being hoarded, and why. There are whole libraries of old literature with barely any relation to the consciousness of a living human. Unread homilies and heroic plays sit in cold storage just in case anyone should think of a reason to look at them. Nobody asks for most of these items anymore.

The screen of the word processor is a space that exists for the sake of revision. Documents are named so they can be modified. The classics (defined as read-only documents it is forbidden to alter) amount to little more than bundles of inert electrons. Such vestigial files are rarely consulted because they show none of those traces of movement – of revision, updating, reformatting – that in an electronic world are the signs of life. Inert information decays. Saving the immortal tapes from that degradation becomes a job with appeal only for glorified clerks, obsessive archivists with a fetish for stasis. It's fundamentally boring, but somebody has to preserve specimens of worn-out genres and obsolete media: triolets and 78s, hagiographies and eight-track tapes, existentialist novels and Betamax videos.

The Magical Custodians

THE CUSTODIAN of the archival tapes is the last to inherit the privileged role of keeper of the books. The file clerk, the librarian, the mad pedant devoting decades to an unfinishable treatise on an arcane point of grammar: each stands in, like an actor in a pageant (a pageant fallen on such hard times that it can now only recruit half-trained part-timers) for the earlier figures of hermit and sage and magician. In one way or another, spells will continue to be hidden in bundles, holy narratives to be kept out of sight when not in ceremonial use, powerful names to be occulted. The keeper of the books bestows and conceals, preserves and imprisons the documents in which energies are sealed:

* The theological prosecutor maintains files on heretical doctrines and the identifying marks of necromancy, files in which he ends up taking a hobbyist's innocent pleasure.
* The gentleman antiquarian in his tower somewhere in the south of England pores over land deeds and etymologies.
* The bishop builds a cabinet with trick locks for his folio of erotic engravings copied from the walls of Pompeii.

* The impoverished scholar-poet, his books half devoured by insects and rough weather, has learned to supply from memory or imagination the gaps in Lucan or Tasso.

* The commissar, with his private collection of confiscated decadent literature, secretly keeps alive the tonalities of Huysmans and Loüys and Gide in the Stalinist night.

* The retired postal worker opens a used-book store off Second Avenue just to give himself an excuse to sit at the back of the store and talk about books all day — books about politics, books about opera, books by James Huneker and Lafcadio Hearn and Carl Van Vechten — with anyone who walks in, a floating conclave of impoverished, sometimes emaciated initiates of the word.

Collectors dwell most on what eludes collection. The keepers of the books are oppressed by dreams of the volumes just out of reach, the ones they can never read or hold. Each has imagined himself the protagonist of a fantastic tale, the one about the book with fatal consequences (as in Robert Chambers's *The King in Yellow,* where its corrupting spirit can be traced along a trail of evil destinies, or Leo Perutz's *The Master of the Day of Judgment,* where it lures century after century of readers to suicide), the book whose subtle poison emanates among the circle of devotees who protect it even as it drains their vitality, whose letters encode the life energy of those named in it, and whose evil influence can be undone not by mere physical destruction – since the idea of the book, the principle of its arrangement, will persist and can always be replicated – but by a literary rearrangement of its contents, an anagrammatic revolution that reverses the effect and turns it in upon itself: the book is forced to read itself, and dies (that is to say, it becomes unreadable).

The libraries are haunted by a further, invisible library: the book written by a man already dead; the book dictated by Silver Birch, an American Indian spirit reaching from beyond the veil to impart to an Edwardian amanuensis his message of world peace; the book dictated from Atlantis, dictated from space; the book that Poe wrote of in "The Man of the Crowd" that "does not permit itself to be read"; the treatise consulted by the protagonist of de Maupassant's "Le Horla" concerning "the unknown inhabitants of the ancient and modern world"; the chronicle written by many hands in which the same mysterious individual appears at wide intervals (say, every hundred years), thereby corroborating an impossible longevity; the book that appears on the shelf with no known provenance and tells of things that have not yet happened (everyone who reads it encounters a different book, the story of his own destiny); the book that tells of past crimes, a different one for each person; the book that, like Paolo and Francesca's, incites to a fatal transgression; the book whose madness is contagious, or the book so sorrowful that whoever reads it loses the will to live; the book into which the reader is drawn so that when he looks up from his reading he is in the room or the parallel reality described therein; or, finally, the book whose insidious urgings turn the reader into a murderer. The last, of course, is not fantastic; more than a few are on file.

If there are no books, there can be no magic books. It is not yet known if there can be such a thing as a magic computer file. There can be hidden files, secret files, confidential files, dangerous files, files for which people would commit heinous crimes. Can there be a file of which they will dream at night for a period of years, or a file at the mention of whose code name they will stop in their tracks as if it forced them, at a moment's notice, to reconsider the pattern of their lives?

Remnants

A MOMENT AGO they were dancing on that spot.

I felt I had gone as far as reading would take me.

And now the book in front of me seems to turn to water. I watch it flow away. The sentences are ripples that break up into foam as I read them. I try to memorize them in a hurry before they change shape, like a species of cloud-writing. So casually the messengers alight, and so quick and unannounced they depart forever.

Not without leaving some trace. They leave behind words. But even if the words remain on the page, I may not ever read them again in quite the same way. I will scan that passage vainly in search of what I once saw there, in a precious vanished minute. What could be more haunting than the absence of what one still possesses?

Because, after all, a book is nothing more than the secondhand imprint of a voice, the voice of a living creature. I look for those voices that can say the unsayable in books that can, at best, show which way they went. The letter kills.

The sentences at hand say the sayable, again and again.

"There is astonishment at the door." "The marquise went out at five o'clock." "All Gaul is divided into three parts." "Near the source of the Seltz, on the left bank of the Rhine some leagues from the imperial city of Worms, there begins a range of mountains." "For many years the use of Portland cement had been growing, until in the early years of the present century it had become the world's chief building material." "These tribes have a great body of romance, in which the actors are animals, and the knowledge of these stories is the lore of their sages." "The first indispensable requisite of happiness is a clear conscience unsullied by the reproach or remembrance of an unworthy action." "A hut is constructed with loose stones, ranged for the most part with some tendency to circularity." "There were many that wandered up and down and were active in sowing discontents and seditions, by venomous and secret murmurings." "The children grow up in every home, naked and dirty, to that strength of limb and size of body which excite our admiration." "And he made his son pass through the fire, and observed times, and used enchantments, and dealt with familiar spirits and wizards." "When he moved his lips, fire blazed forth." "The gods cowered like dogs and crouched in distress." "My eye is sun and my breath is wind, air is my soul and earth my body." "The gods are later than this world's production."

The uncanniness I associate with the experience of

reading is not *in* the sentences, but it was the sentences that made me aware of it. It is under them, or between them, or analogous to them, or parallel to them. It emerges in their vicinity, but only for as long as one's back is turned. It floats nearby, or did so recently enough to have left this barely perceptible residue, a faint trace that is yet the gist, the only finally real aspect of what I'm caught up in. It is a dance of spirit entering husk, spirit leaving husk, and much of the time there is only husk and the word is nothing more than a word and there are too many of them, a huge cemetery full of language.

Does the uncanniness surrounding the sentences reside only in the fact that they continue to speak in the absence of a speaker, that they are live speech a dead man hid? Does the ancient book instill a quiet fear because its language is dead or because, on the contrary, it communicates a recognizable voice? Which is more terrible, death or resurrection?

The Lost World

IT IS A QUESTION OF how much one can hope to find. To discover for the first time what was written by those now dead will be another birth, but of what? Will the dismembered god live again when the story is told? Is not the promise in the prophet's sealed-up scroll simply of novelty value, a fresh twist on an old formula, metaphors and parables never before available in stores? But they will be readable only to the extent that they tell me what I have already been told. The genres of ultimate truth-telling – prophecy, lyric, devotion – are too familiar, by now as readily recognizable in their structures and strategies as the murder ballad, the riddle, or the wedding hymn. Even the birth of the universe – or rather, especially the birth of the universe – is a commonplace. Heraldries and sacred symbols can be bought like packs of playing cards.

The only oracle with truly startling information is the one I can't decipher, the one whose inscribers (it is permissible to imagine) may have had words for matters that no one else knew about, words that as a result would be untranslat-

able even if we could transliterate them. The rest of it –
floodwater, tree, eye, wound, gift, stain, feather – I have
translated, as it were, in advance, with the aid of a preselect-
ed menu of meanings, the private vocabulary that like every
other reader I have appropriated from the public language.

What I can possess is not the intangible but the grossly
material, these blocks, these rotting weights, these cushions
leaking air over a period of centuries, these shards of board
stuck with remnants of contradictory messages. Is it because
of some perceived inadequacy of the words I already hold in
my hand that I am compelled to keep digging deeper in the
dust in which I'm already knee-deep, flinging the available,
overfamiliar words aside to look for other more desirable
words, hunting for the undiscovered work that must persist
somewhere down there, in the form of a scroll, a sheaf of
manuscripts, a papyrus rolled up in a jar waiting to be stumbled upon by some scavenging well-digger of the twenty-
third century? By that time it might be any book, of course;
it might be the one I am reading right now. On the other
hand, I cannot know if these words I'm reading will be
among those lost forever, if indeed any person will ever read
them again.

It's a matter of blind luck that any book survives at all.
Tacitus would be lost if not for a solitary ninth-century Car-
olingian copyist, and Caesar and Livy as well. The burned
books of pagan and Gnostic philosophers survive, in copious

but piecemeal quotation, amid the paragraphs of those who refuted them. The anti-Christian Platonist Celsus persists as illustrative material in the rejoinders of Origen, the Gnostics live on in their theological enemy Irenaeus, as if the murderer were condemned to preserve his victim, or as if the words of the victim issued from the mouth of his devourer.

How extravagantly fortuitous to have so much as a copy of a copy of a copy. It would be churlish to complain that you can never be altogether sure if the sole surviving transcript resembles in any way the original of which it claims to be a copy. The original is as dead and dissolved as Julius Caesar or Mark Antony, and *they* are so far gone that it becomes grotesque to think that such persons could ever have had the temerity to exist, to *be* Caesar or Antony. What pale replicas must those living bodies have been, compared to the density of the shadows into which language has transformed them, the shadows that have ricocheted back and forth so many times. It as if they become more real, more profoundly rooted in what they really are, the farther they get from their almost arbitrary fleshly source. Will the books likewise seem more real when we are no longer able to read them?

THE WORDS THAT SURVIVE are only a haunting reminder of other words that were lost. Their very survival exacerbates the craving for what is irremediably absent, as if we would willingly sacrifice everything we know for only a peek at what we don't. Our luck is what we know; our misfortune is what we don't even have an inkling of not knowing. Can those sentences really have vanished and left no residue?

That the books die, disappear, are made to disappear: that certainty is the shadow side of reading. The book read is haunted by the book unread, unreadable, lost or untranslated, deliberately destroyed or accidentally mislaid: Harpocration's *Collection of Florid Expressions* or Suetonius's *Greek Grammar* and *The Lives of Famous Whores* and *The Physical Defects of Mankind* (lost through the ravages of time), Margaret Fuller's history of the Italian revolution (lost at sea), the second book of Gogol's *Dead Souls* (burnt by the author), the memoirs of Byron and the diaries of Sir Richard Burton (burnt after the authors' death for the sake of propriety), the final chapters of *The Mystery of Edwin Drood* (these last longed for so profoundly that psychics have been employed to retrieve them from the ether).

The books themselves tell us of the death of books, of the wars waged indiscriminately against people and against books. To destroy a single book is as good as erasing whole generations of transmitted thoughts. In the writings of Chia Yi we learn how the first Ch'in emperor "discarded the ways of the former kings and burned the writings of the hundred schools in order to make the people ignorant." Ammianus Marcellinus tells us in the twenty-ninth book of his history how, in the reign of Emperor Valens, a hunt after sorcerers and treasonous prophets turned into a wholesale gutting of libraries: "Then innumerable books and whole heaps of documents, which had been routed out from various houses, were piled up and burnt under the eyes of the judges. They were treated as forbidden texts to allay the indignation caused by the executions, though most of them were treatises on various liberal arts and on jurisprudence." But these were as nothing to the unmanageable catalogue of parchments and scrolls that have shriveled into ashes in every invasion, every civil war, from England to Japan, from monasteries burned by warlords to monasteries sacked by Vikings.

It would be foolish to imagine that some aspect of the work might persist even if it dissolves completely, that the libraries of antiquity, the lost plays of Aeschylus or Sophocles, the complete Sappho, continue to exert influence on some arcane, essentially imperceptible level. They don't. Books without readers are not books, particularly if they do not contain any words. And yet, and yet: the idea of an idea of them does somehow continue to exert pressure. If we can believe that such an echo remains audible, there may be hope for the analogous survival of some wisp of our own being. There is a thread of possibility in the notion that those who read those lost books told others of them, and those others told others, and that thus some portion of their contents (however unidentifiable, however dissipated and transformed) has been preserved by oral transmission. Indeed, how could it not be? But which sentences bear the traces?

If not in books or spoken sentences, one might look in people for such remnants. The ancient reader absorbed a text so completely that he embodied it, becoming what could be called a walking gospel or sutra. That might be the inner structure of a lost dynastic ode that his remote descendant is so casually exhaling. The very air that Antony breathed escapes on all sides. Somebody is still unwittingly carrying on a pretty good imitation of his shuffle.

Doctor Tobacco

THE SENTENCES ESCAPE, but where? To a book. They go into a book to reassemble their scattered bodies, to take a breather, to figure out what they're *doing*. They go there in order to become true. Truth would be a condition in which the words stopped moving around. I have had the impression more than once of opening such a book, and finding that it contained the truth as absolutely as a clay vessel contains water. It was the book I had been hoping to find, the book the stories about books were about. Not many books but one, a final one, like the war to end all wars.

People used to have dreams like this in the Middle Ages, with every object clearly marked off: there was The Chamber and The Window and The Bird Feeder, The Garden Gate and The Vestibule and The Reading Desk. It was upon The Reading Desk that The Book was spread open. It may even have been attached to it by a chain. This was to signify that truth cannot be illicitly apprehended.

I too had longed for such a book. Was it because I was discontented with being a reader? Did I want reading to be something more and other than itself, some impossible encounter with a book that would be, like a living person, capable of dialogue; able to speak for itself without letting words, even the words of which it was composed, get in the way; a book that would say what it's saying, instead of just saying it without saying so?

I can no longer remember any of the words in that book but I remember that simply from how they looked on the page – even without reading them – I could recognize a verbal diagram of the structure of reality. It was like a dream about a skeleton in which you know – without close examination, and in utter ignorance of the science of anatomy – that every detail is precise and in its place. I forget what this volume was called, something like *The Nature of Being* or *Thoughts as Objects* or *The Poetics of Meaning*.

THE AUTHOR WAS A BEING of unusual profundity – sometimes familiarly referred to as Doctor Tobacco. His life was a matter of conjecture and legend: a poverty that from some angles seemed self-imposed, eccentric bursts of temper and generosity, long fallow periods devoted to repetitive manual tasks. No image of his face existed, a deliberate refusal on his part. He had, some said, only ever read some six or seven books, but he had read them as nothing had ever been read before and from them had deduced the gist of all the other volumes. He had the rare capacity to suggest that, in the very act of reading, it was he and not I who was doing the reading: I merely assisted, as an audience, at his reading of his own treatise. Or was it that the place inside himself from which he wrote existed within anyone, so that his text had the virtue of putting me in the position to realize that I myself had written it?

It was an odd kind of novel he had written. The characters were eyeballs, premises, rays, question marks. Abstractions underwent adventures, in a deadpan manner worthy of a magnificent and almost arrogantly proud clown or prestidigitator. The neatest trick played by these abstractions was to prove – through a sequence of acrobatic hairsplitting contortions – that they had never existed in the first place. But that was just the punch line of one episode. In the next one, the point might be that any one of them was the same as any other; or that the sum total of their flailing and somersaulting was something called God. All that the Doctor could do in words amounted to a sudden wrench or tweak, an act that, while implying all the violence that could ever be committed, effected no real harm.

It occurred on such a night as this, now that it has gotten dark and I walk again among the thoughts of the dead keeper of the manor where I first came upon that book. Again I peer with a certain cautiousness down the encrusted passageway at whose mouth a squadron of cobwebbed nouns stands sentry in honor of deceased sovereigns. The courtyard is full of cold machines. Yet the sentence's engine, however rusted, coughs into movement. The whirring and clanking reverberate through the boards and panels of the deserted mansion.

The ghost of argument walks abroad. There are spirits in the bushes who discourse of zodiac and volition. A grand ballet of monads takes place in the empty ballroom. They leapfrog over one another with courtly slowness; they deploy themselves in the form of proofs. Every dancer is a thought. Logical extensions shoot from the main shapes like branches. The discarded shells of used thoughts pile up like dried husks on a forest floor, flung aside as if there were no hope they might live again. Marks of death, nothing more, nothing usable; and this was the place I had mistaken for a house in which one might live.

It is in the pages of the philosopher-novelist Doctor Tobacco that we can best take inventory of the contents of the abandoned manor house. With selfless rigor he applied to that heap of mouldering furniture the most ancient of mnemonic techniques. The first mode of being is in the cupboard, the second mode of being is on the shelf, the third mode of being is under the bed, and at the same time they are all in the steward's bedchamber and therefore one, yet because it is the steward's and not the lord's room these modes are in truth inferior definitions, subsumed under the larger and grander category with which the master bedroom is entrusted. Doctor Tobacco locks himself in a room so he can hear what he is thinking while he ticks off every stairwell and cabinet and skylight of the Palace of Memory.

The house is a grammar. Within its rooms he contemplates the parts of speech. This time, as if for the first time, as if no one had ever thought of doing such a thing, he will sort through them and see what they really consist of, what they have really been doing all this time while people thought they were doing something else. He will find out, in short, what the people were actually saying as opposed to what they only imagined they were saying. He will prove that each word is distinct; and then on a different day he will prove that the words are nonetheless interchangeable. In the end, the attempt to reconcile the two notions makes something snap inside him.

One afternoon, at length, he seizes on the idea that each word is a hole into which can be – and probably have been – poured an infinity of meanings, associations, lives, worlds. Almost anything can be extracted from any one of them, from *justice* or *knob* or *knee* or *veer* – and, without question, from *letter* or *grove* or *quarrel* or *salvage* – and, why not, *savage* and *save* and *solve* and *solvent*? He makes a note: "Meaning leaks from words as life leaks from our bodies." That is the afternoon when he begins to draft the book I have been reading.

"Language must be empowered to abolish language": a

character in one of his dialogues makes this assertion. Elsewhere another speaker declares: "I have never laid eyes on a single concept." These personas behave as if recovering from shock, as if some impression they had received of the real nature of language had reduced them to a sort of hermetic bluntness: "I must tell you that nothing can be told. This is not the same as saying that lies are true, or that people cannot do otherwise than lie. Yet the eyes see perfectly well even in the absence of written sentences, the walls stand, the breeze picks up." This is why it was necessary to empty the linguistic system of meaning: so as not to have a headache on a fine morning, especially when Doctor Tobacco has been up all night writing sentences that do not altogether preclude the existence of a perfect Negative Beauty.

He walks out into the yard and lights his first cigarette of the day. "Speech that declares the desirability of silence," he says to no one, "is not the same as merely keeping silent, but the very opposite." A few steps take him to the well for a cup of cold water. "Silence is mute oppression unless it is deliberate, and it is necessary to say so. It is necessary to say that one intends to be silent."

SOME YEARS LATER — it took a while for word of his researches to get around — soldiers show up at the inn with orders for his immediate arrest. The problem is the sentence about silence, a sentence that in the published version of his treatise is a footnote, as unobtrusive as he could make something on which the structure of his book depended. Everything would have been all right if he had simply argued that it was sufficient in some cases to refrain from speech. It would have been possible to go on for centuries like that, as people sometimes do.

Doctor Tobacco finds himself in prison. They are going to interrogate him, torture him perhaps, until he reveals what they already know. They, of course, are readers too, close readers, indeed the closest of all since a hair's difference in interpretation is with them a matter of blood. I want to affirm (uselessly, given my distance from his place of imprisonment) that he is the most harmless of men, this philosopher. Except that to say so would carry the humiliating implication that he has wasted his life on frivolities, on texts that could just as easily have read slightly differently. Change a no to a yes and everything is fine. Is he really going to have to die for a footnote?

The Cemetery of the Ancestors

THE CHIEF INTERROGATOR, to my surprise, turns out to be Inspector French, that most reasonable of men. The inspector is fond of travel and a good pint, and is known in the department for his aversion to backbiting and political maneuvering. He hasn't, it's true, much of a flair for aesthetic distinctions, although he is capable of admiring the sheer craftsmanship, not to mention stamina, embodied in a carved church door in Souillac or a fine old brewery in Southwold. Nor is he much of a reader; he hasn't actually plowed through Doctor Tobacco's treatise, but has glanced at a rather good résumé (prepared by the authoritative, highly secretive Readers Committee) in which the disputed points — relatively few at bottom — are set forth in terse bulleted recaps. "You see," he says with a bit of twinkle, "just between us, silence in law is a bit of a gray area. If you'd said nothing at all that would probably have been fine; but to draw attention to the fact puts the whole thing on a different footing. Once you've done that, you convert even complete inactivity into a sort of statement. A man might keep his mouth shut and speak volumes, and nobody would be the wiser: very troubling from our point of view, as I'm sure you can understand."

The philosopher is in hot water because his mode of silence opens up a territory incapable of regulation. It's too wide, too blank. The Readers Committee has devoted a number of meetings to this subject, meetings whose upshot is invariably some form of judicial violence, at the very least some form of incarceration or deletion. Their business is simply to keep dictionaries functional, and the implications of that trade are intrinsically rough. They themselves are not really in it for the rough stuff; they take a genuine pleasure in the theoretical problems that arise constantly in their work.

But they would never deny the violence that must be done to a word to make it specify, the harsh restraints to which it must be subjected to keep it from wriggling away from its designated meaning. The *lien* and *tenure* and *estate* of the harshest of jargons, the words that bind and divest and dispossess, the vocabulary list from which law books are made and that empowers all forms of ligature and chastisement: in, on, or about such words is where language strains at its limits, marshals to the fullest its capacity to nail down. "The letter killeth": this is that letter. Only certain kinds of words and statements are permissible, and only certain interpretations can be made of them. Any shift in the definition of a word constitutes a revolution. The language of law, by limiting itself, limits those who use it or about whom it is used. The committee members are patrol guards in the war of the words. It is not enough to have a sacred text; there must be only one way to read it.

Otherwise something precious escapes. The loss of a cherished meaning is a kind of death, more wrenching even than the death of a person. That people are born and die, we know; that they are born and die within a vocabulary that resists change we sincerely hope. Language is the consecrated ground in which our ancestors are buried. For the hope that a word can have strict and durable meaning, for that insane hope, scrolls are ripped apart and bridges set on fire.

And all because the isolated words, at the end, are all there is. One must pray they have a consistency that those who use them lack. The words contain truth that rebounds on those who construct lies out of them. The words guard their own meaning. They persist like genetic instructions. We are told things by them but can never know as much as they know.

Otherwise something precious oozes beyond one's grasp. The connection a person makes between one word and another all by itself makes a basis for a new religion or a new war. Someone comes to realize that he is prepared to die, or at least kill, for the sake of a fragment of a remembered poem: "river-colored dawn" or "the soil's sob" or "long line of willows." The history of how he learned to talk becomes a visit to the graves of his cousins. He is himself the tomb of language. Liturgy is chain mail, dictionary is family tree. Merely by pronouncing the commonest words, he perpetuates the memory of exile and massacre, until to speak is to incite reprisal.

No need to be born into such a history. It can be assumed as if by accident, in a moment of apparent inattention. This is what happened to the protagonist's father in Charles Brockden Brown's novel *Wieland:*

> One Sunday afternoon, being induced to retire for a few minutes to his garret, his eye was attracted by a page of this book, which, by some accident, had been opened and placed full in his view. He was seated on the edge of his bed, and was employed in repairing a rent in some part of his clothes. His eyes were not confined to his work, but occasionally wandering, lighted at length upon the page. The words "Seek and ye shall find," were those that first offered themselves to his notice.

As light as a feather floating down toward a hard surface is the movement of the reader's mind approaching the words that will take irrevocable possession of it.

The secluded scholar little dreams how far his search will take him. Gradually he begins to gauge how inextricable are the patterns that waited only for his eye to pick them out from the camouflaging mass of irrelevant detail – if, indeed, any detail can truly be irrelevant to such a scholar's eye. Hopping from cross-reference to cross-reference, tracking each allusion to its lair, checking every alibi and unmasking every pseudonym, he will find the path to the solution of all the mysteries: the secret projects of the Order of Templars, the fate of the ghost ship *Marie Celeste* and of the Roanoke colony, the facts that make nonsense of the single-bullet theory, the disappearance of Judge Crater, the suppressed clauses of the Lourdes revelation, the identity of Kaspar Hauser, and the truth about the man in the iron mask.

It waited only for him. Time is full. It sounds at this moment, the appointed hour for the predestined agent to get to the bottom of fifty centuries of disinformation and altered testimony. Cooked books! False gospels! Diabolically reversed hymnals! Misattributed quotes and downright plagiarism! History written by the victors! The treason of the clerks! Deliberate mislabeling to ensure that documents get lost forever in the files! Substitution of forgeries for the purloined originals! Concoction ex nihilo of whole libraries of seditious slander! He will prove they lied even if he has to lie to do so.

But there's no need to lie: it's all here, it never went away. The old allegations wash up on the same island and they are rescued inexorably by one castaway after another. It's all here, like new: canards hatched by disinherited aristos of the 1790s find new soil in the brains of anxious farmers and overqualified filing clerks. We know who "they" are and we have the footnotes to prove it. They are the Masons, the Illuminati, the Rosicrucians, the Jews, the Jacobins, the freethinkers, the bankers, the Bolsheviks, the homosexuals. All of them one thing in the end: so many aliases to hide a single dark name.

And against the bearer of that name the inquisitorial reader finds the energy to pronounce a cherished anathema, grateful that he can abandon himself to the act of pronouncing it:

> May he be accursed in eating and drinking, in waking and sleeping, in coming and going. Accursed be he in living and dying; may his vocation be sinful, and his days be few and evil; may his substance be enjoyed by others, and his children be orphans, and his wife a widow. May his children be ever in need, and may none help them; may they be turned out of their home and their goods taken by usurers; and may they find nobody to have compassion on them; and may his children's children be ruined and outcast, and their names also. May their enemies vanquish them and despoil them of all they possess in the world; and may they wander from door to door without relief.

The fervent, potentially fanatical reader grants himself permission to be converted. He has an inkling of what the words will say even before they say it. He kicks them as he would a horse, to spur them on. They are not enlightening him quickly enough, he races ahead of them, some part of him begins to despise them for not being even more brutal and absolute than they are. He relishes being carried at high speed to the heart of the hunt, careful above all not to let himself be thrown. He will not be cowed by the words or found wanting by them. Anything they can throw at him he's ready for. He will be as tough and unforgiving as they are.

Or else, moving his lips over their steely configurations, he will come to feel that the sentences love him. It can happen anywhere: encountering the word *gate* or *fountain* in an advertisement for religion on the subway, or the phrase *comprador class* or *practical philosophy* in the pages of an academic quarterly devoted to political science. Every cult, every terrorist cell begins as a vocabulary list. Systematic projects of extermination are rooted in bibliography. Once the novitiate has learned how to understand an old word in a new way, he is ready to begin. He has become part of the argument.

Close Readers

CLOSE READING IS MANDATORY in the fallen world. So often the text has been written under duress and is planted with coded messages from a captive author. Doctor Tobacco's book, for instance, took shape in a society where many things were impossible to say, and thus the author was obliged to use arcane symbols to impart his message secretly and selectively. But suppose the reader is not the liberator of the author's imprisoned meaning but the captor looking for signs of escape attempts and secret protests?

The author involuntarily betrays himself, lays out his secrets one by one. His own words will be turned against him; the reader is compiling evidence to bring against him at a tribunal. Authorship, in this light, is nothing but the mark of trespass.

From a slightly different vantage point, the author is not evil, really, just sick. He has become ill, not all at once but by the gradual accumulation of debilitating failures and wrong turns. His work has made him ill. It falls to the reader to come up with a way to help him, to get him out of his trap, force him to change or at least to undergo some preliminary tests, perhaps a short period of hospitalization. For who more intimately than the reader can come to know the weakness of the author, his quirks of evasion, his endless tricks of misdirection and impersonation?

The reader I have in mind – the reader I can feel at moments reading over my shoulder, and who I sometimes fear I could become – might be a hypochondriac who sees the text as a potential vector of infection. The sickness or evil of the writer is transmissible; or, even if the writer is essentially blameless, whatever evil or sickness he touches upon in the way of subject matter is catching.

There are forbidden names, names that by being sounded call up demons, words that by being glimpsed spread fevers through the arms and legs. In the first place they are forbidden because of what they do; in the second place because of what is done to those who come in contact with them. Even if the unfortunate reader was not aware that he had been corrupted, the words he can be proved to have read prove him wrong. He was lost from the moment he opened the book to a particular page, like that king who was poisoned by a powder smeared across the letters of an illuminated manuscript.

The reader as incipient prosecutor is initiated into the great school of suspicion. Trained to read fearfully, he finds that the fear rebounds upon him. He begins to be afraid, for example, that his own reading will be inadequate, that he will draw the wrong conclusion. To illustrate the fear, he proposes to himself an example of a wrong conclusion: If a sacred book can exist, how can any book not be sacred? How different could any book be, if it were written in the same human language? Of necessity it would use the same *the,* the same *of* and *and:* if the whole is sacred, then the parts that make it up must be sacred. To suggest that a mere human word could profane the sacred presumes, with all too human vanity, that the sacred can in such fashion be profaned.

He is afraid that if he continues in this vein he will suffer a fate like that of the priest who was damned because he doubted for only one instant, while the murdering bandit was raised on high because for a crucial half second he believed he would be saved. If the signs may be so easily reversed, then blasphemy can masquerade as benison, or benison as blasphemy.

He had not understood before how terrifying a book can be. The text may be a prophecy in which he is going to learn something unbearable about the future. Eventually he will come to know – indeed, has he not known it all along? – that the text is about himself. He is read by what he reads. The book knows exactly at what point he is going to recoil from what is written there. For the book, if it knows nothing else, knows what the reader will find; it is already there, waiting for him. It knows the reader's future because it is that future.

A Meditation on Reading

It is the reader who has done wrong. Did the book teach him that, or was it his guilty knowledge that drove him to the book in the first place? He goes over the text, nervously checking to see if the author has assembled enough evidence to convict him. So consumed is he with a sense of wrongdoing that he imagines himself nailed time and again. Each sentence has been written in order to lay bare his faults to the reading public.

He will be brought to book by this book that is nothing less than a body of evidence, a painstaking compilation of obscure sins, small acts of cruelty and avarice, the failure to answer a letter, the inability to recognize in a crowd the face of a former lover, the withholding of a word of comfort from a dying stranger.

The Blasphemers

Finally, sentence is passed, in secret, and Doctor Tobacco is sequestered for what might as well be forever. Time takes on a different meaning under these circumstances. But since ways must still be found to occupy it, he finds his way to the prison library. Even if he reads one volume a day, he will not get to the end of them before his sentence is up. He will not get to the end of them, in fact, even if they never let him out.

And so he reads. To give himself a sense of order, of progression, he reads according to plan: starting on the top left shelf in the first room of the library, he will read each book in order, moving from left to right, then each of the shelves in that bookcase, before repeating the process with each of the bookcases in turn, with each of the rooms in turn. The books are in no discernible order, but he accepts their random distribution as another kind of pattern, no less valid than one dictated by theme or chronology or the alphabet.

The pattern has to do with duration, the time it will take

him to read his way through this library. He measures his life by sentences and chapters. He comes to feel that just as any moment of life contains the whole of it, any of these books is the whole library, any sentence the whole book. This realization affords him enormous relief. To allow himself to be lost in this reading is his salvation.

As he reads, it's as if all the books were one, a single big book into which all the little books coalesce, resembling a multigenerational novel into which all possible incidents of a lifetime are packed. *The Blasphemers:* "A saga pulsing with human emotion, tumultuous and absorbing!" *The Blasphemers:* "An edge-of-your-seat drama of ambition, treachery, and passion!" *The Blasphemers:* "With their bare hands they carved an empire out of a savagely beautiful wilderness!" *The Blasphemers:* "They played to win in a game where the stakes were love and death!" *The Blasphemers:* "They took what they wanted – and they wanted it all!"

The episodes of this novel move him more than he could have believed possible in that remote other life when he wondered how a single sentence could say anything at all. Now it seems rather as if any sentence says, promiscuously, everything. So his days are passed advancing through the thousand or more pages of a paperbound book so monstrously thick that his life may well end before the story does.

It is as if he has simply become part of that small town in the France of 1780 a country ripe for upheaval and full of simple objects such as baskets horseshoes and knives where notaries wear wigs and doctors put leeches on the sick and in whose public square the marquis takes a horsewhip to a surly groom while the groom's young son who is really a foundling abandoned at birth on the church steps watches and seethes with rage vowing that when he grows up he will have his revenge on these decadent rulers afflicted with gout and myopia and pounding his fist against the wall for emphasis while he shouts that people weren't meant to live like this like dogs we live like dogs he can calm himself only by remembering his love for the blacksmith's beautiful daughter who has been his intended bride since childhood so much so that everything else in their lives has seemed merely prelude to the moment when they will become one except that the blacksmith owes money to the marquis and the marquis in turn owes money a great deal of money to the local banker an elderly and unhealthy man inexorable in the punishment of debtors who connives at a fiendish deal whereby the marquis will forgive the blacksmith's debt if the blacksmith will give his daughter in marriage to the banker the banker in turn forgiving the marquis's debt in exchange for the marquis's using his more or less feudal authority to force acceptance of an arrangement all too typical of pre-revolutionary France so that the blacksmith's daughter marries the banker driving the groom's son so wild with rage that he climbs into their house and abducts the bride on her wedding night riding off with her into the forested wilderness that existed at that time in southern France and when a storm comes on they take shelter in the ruins of an old monastery closely connected with a local scandal concerning a monk outstanding for his piety and asceticism who broke his vows by seducing the young sister of the marquis and then abandoning her after getting her with child so that the girl hanged herself after giving birth and the fate of the child from that day to this remained unknown and consequently the monk was expelled by the abbot but came back in the night and set fire to the monastery with the monks inside so incinerating all of them in a single night and then disappeared forever into the forest where according to the local peasants he still wanders working evil on passing strangers and when the lovers take shelter they discover the ruin is the hideout for notorious bandits who have been terrorizing the surrounding region a discovery confirmed by the arrival of these bandits led by none other than the accursed monk now a monster of cruelty attended by hirelings no less cruel who intend as a matter of course to kill the lovers who have stumbled on their refuge except that the groom's son challenges the monk and the bandits are impressed by his spirit being frankly a little weary of the monk's arbitrary rages and so the groom's son and the monk fight to the death the monk being fatally wounded in the contest but noticing as he expires a peculiar birthmark on the shoulder of the groom's son reveals with his dying breath that the foundling is the son born from the forbidden liaison of the monk and the sister of the marquis in the wake of which revelation the bandits proclaim the stunned youth their chief and he accedes to the role with grace proceeding to harass the landowners of the region especially the marquis his own uncle who had horsewhipped his foster father except that by now the French Revolution has arrived and the marquis himself is in jeopardy is in fact betrayed by his own son a malignant and avaricious character only too happy to betray his father to the revolutionaries and thereby establish his credentials with the local branch of the Jacobin party with whose connivance and under cover of pursuing the Jacobin policy of terror he turns the Revolution into a gigantic land-grab except that the bandit chief who is of course the cousin of the marquis's son has taken up the cause of royalism and has converted his bandits into patriotic guerrilla fighters fighting a vicious small-scale war against the forces led by the Jacobin cousin a war that turns into an extended game of cat and mouse and finally takes the bandit chief and his bride into the rugged mountains where the lovers make their last stand so that in the very region where the Albigensian heretics were once brought to heel by the Catholic armies of the north the outlaw and his love confront the naked force of another Parisian government a struggle that can end only one way with the lovers going up memorably in flames except that prior to this the abducted bride has given birth to twins a boy and a girl Lucien and Marianne who on their parents' death fall into the hands of the son of the marquis and are raised with no clue to their original identity except for identical necklaces given to them by their mother family heirlooms going back to the Visigothic warlords who were their ancestors and by now it is turning into the nineteenth century which means that affairs are going to become even more complex and secretive the children will be separated and will lose their names and their social standing after the son of the marquis comes to the bad and brutal end incurred through his evil dealings during the Revolution a cataclysm that leads to the children being scattered to opposite ends of Europe the girl Marianne to become an actress legendary for her beauty the boy Lucien to become a mercenary apt for any adventure who finds his destiny in the corrupt power centers of the east among czarist officials and leering emirs in a region where many bad things happen sieges scenes of torture slave markets pirate raids where he will go hungry for months in a Saracen prison only to escape and follow the trail of an old map into the Siberian forest where he will discover gold returning to civilization covered with medals for having subdued the natives and brought wealth to the empire an accomplishment so glorious that the czar sends him out on another expedition this time to explore the northwest coast of America during which expedition he's shipwrecked and washed ashore in northern California where the dark-haired daughter of a local hidalgo cares for him and from their secret love a child is born a trespass that leads to disaster when the hidalgo a man obsessed with the honor of his name discovers what has happened and fights a duel with the Russian explorer in which both are killed after which the girl mad with grief flees into the desert with her newborn daughter and while all this is going on Lucien's sister Marianne heads west to London where her natural vivacity makes her the toast of the theater world an accomplished if instinctive actress who in short order is the mistress of a count and then a king and emerges ultimately as a political conspirator with a Machiavellian eye for the main chance consumed with a desire to avenge the wrongs of the past and to reclaim the ancestral lands of which she feels she has been defrauded lands that have long since passed into the hands of that banker from whom her mother was abducted a man whom she now in her new identity seeks to destroy utterly through a scheme of entrapment involving forged bank certificates calculated to involve him in a public humiliation so complete that self-inflicted death is the only way out but not before he has queered the deal for her by implicating her in turn in a murder she could almost have committed forcing her to flee further west to America where she's swept up in the colorful life of New York from the rat-infested harbor swarming with cutpurses and madwomen to the exclusive clubs where an already decadent elite pursues its vices a city where she plays out the hand that's left to her until she winds up feverish and half-deranged smoking opium to relieve both physical pain and her infinite regret for what she left behind in the old country not to mention her misgivings on behalf of her two illegitimate children a son Marcus the offspring of Marianne's misbegotten love for her wastrel lover a patroon's heir gone wrong and destined to perish in a duel and a younger daughter Toinette whose father was a land-grabbing congressman who terrified at the prospect of being forced to acknowledge the child's patrimony will stop at nothing to relieve himself of this blot on his ostensibly blameless character using violent threats to force his cast-off mistress to run for her life with the two children into the wilderness heading as far out into unknown territory as her rapidly failing health will permit barely dragging herself into a border town in time to die that very night so that her children Marcus nearly ten Toinette only four and barely aware of what's going on become charity cases it's the era of the Black Hawk War and not long afterward there's an Indian raid in which the boy Marcus is taken prisoner and spends the next ten years living among the Indians while his sister Toinette becomes the ward of a local preacher a crazed Indian-hater who stirs up violent disorder harping on the boy's fate while unknown to any in the settlement Marcus is being raised by the tribal elders and initiated into their visionary traditions has in fact almost forgotten his own inherited ways when the white people incited by the preacher come to rescue him massacring everybody else in the tribe and haul him back to a civilization where he's a misfit so unsuited for any kind of normal life that as soon as he comes of age he heads back to the wilderness leaving behind a bitterly disappointed sister who can no longer tolerate life with a tyrannical foster father becoming more visibly crazy with every passing year a despot who attempts to control every aspect of her life until she too runs off stowing away on a steamboat and heading downriver to the bright lights of New Orleans where in the French Quarter she becomes the model of a young painter who falls passionately in love with her and with whom living in poverty and among the faded splendors of Creole culture she passes unforgettable months which are only the prelude to a brilliant period when the painter already famous for the ambitious scope of his historical canvases accompanies her to London and Paris and Rome leaving the past behind them including her lost brother who disappears for years into the gold mines and brothels of the far west accumulating a fortune by means that are not always the most honest and in the end founding a virtual empire financed by gold and copper and maintained by brute force with a private army at his beck and call and taking as his bride the most beautiful of all the whores for whom he stages a wedding fiesta whose gaudiness and abandon enters local legend a gesture typical of the expansive energies that make him appear the embodiment of life itself reckless generous brutal yet doomed by the same flaw that led him to marry the wrong woman a vengeful beauty who taunts him with her infidelities and destroys his peace of mind until he spirals down into a stupefied gloom verging on the catatonic from which he emerges only once more abruptly and catastrophically on a hot summer night to strangle her set fire to his estate and blow his brains out leaving behind the ruins of an empire and two young children both boys strangely opposite in character who after the disaster of their parents' end follow drastically different paths Lucas the elder becoming an ambitious politician while Tom the younger pursues the life of a carefree outlaw going to Mex-

ico and selling weapons to peasants and bandits in revolt
against the oppressive landowners at the same time that
Lucas is rising to power in Washington D.C. during the
scandals surrounding the presidency of Ulysses S. Grant
scandals that permit him under the guise of reformism to
take ruthless advantage of the situation and become the
pivotal power broker in the nation's capital a man consumed with imperial dreams who vows to exterminate the
outlaw bands plaguing the far west and hindering eco-
nomic development most especially the band led by the
notorious Tomás who he little suspects is in fact his
younger brother but who embodies the state of simmering
unrest in the far territories the sense of dread sweeping
across the plains attended by visions of violence and impending social collapse an air of anxious anticipation that
finds fulfillment in the legends surrounding a woman said
to possess miraculous healing powers and the gift of
prophecy whose fanatical followers known as the Harrowers of God wish to establish a new state in the midst of the
wilderness a rigid theocracy governed by their high priestess selecting for this purpose a barren region of no apparent interest to other settlers but which turns out to be rich
in gold a discovery that comes to the attention of the outlaw Tomás who worms his way into the sect and is accept-
ed as a Harrower not so difficult a task because they are
grim and taciturn and hardly notice that Tomás doesn't
say much so that everything seems to favor his purpose
until he sees the priestess and conceives for her a passion
so uncontrollable that he abducts her in the midst of the

Harrowers' most important ceremony and takes her to the hills where his band of outlaws awaits and is preparing a forced marriage when he notices that the necklace she wears is identical to one that his grandmother Marianne wore and that has been passed down in the family and realizes that the priestess is really the daughter of his grandmother's brother the czarist adventurer Lucien and the hidalgo's daughter in California who raised in remote mountain areas by her half-crazed mother and subject since childhood to strange dreams and premonitions is nonetheless undeniably his own aunt a fact that once established leads them to stare at each other in mutual astonishment at just the moment that the army led by Lucas arrives on the scene leading to a pitched battle in the course of which the priestess is killed in the crossfire in a scene of such confusion that when the two brothers meet at last face to face they are unable to determine whose bullet was responsible for the death of their aunt a miserable scene in whose aftermath Tomás curses the heavens for laying such a burden on his family a curse that elicits from his sanctimonious brother the cry of blasphemy prompting Tomás to reply that yes we are all destined to be blasphemers but if it must be so let's live our fate to the hilt and so saying plunges a knife into his brother's heart and vanishes again into the wild hills and with that vanishing seems to signal that a whole century a whole way of life is disappearing replaced by a new epoch whose atmosphere is quite different no more Indian wars no more hidalgos the orange groves are linked by rail to every major metropolitan center on the whitewashed walls of the stations murals are painted in which the spirit of civic beauty draped in gauze gathers in her arms the fruits of rural labor and urban capital and in the alleys blackened by factory smoke the workers smoke cigarettes and talk of movies and strikes and lipstick and whiskey a century in which the family with which the story has been concerned almost seems to have become extinct the last surviving line dwindling out as Toinette's children grow up in an ambience of cosmopolitan luxury among the spas and salons of Europe and when Toinette's granddaughter returns to America it's as the wife of a young expatriate painter who has revolutionized modern art with what he calls Yankee Dada and with whom she leads an anarchic and abandoned life in Manhattan until it becomes clear that the painter is not only a genius but also a drug-addicted and obsessively jealous maniac who threatens their young daughter and whom she's forced to kill making it look like an accident and almost getting away with it except that the supercilious art dealer who has already ruthlessly exploited the painter's talents stumbles on evidence that will prove it was really murder thus blackmailing her into becoming his mistress the result being a household that seethes with unspoken hatred and deep misunderstanding the daughter resenting her mother for what she perceives as unfaithfulness to the father's memory until finally the mother breaks down and tells her what really happened shocking the daughter so much that she runs away to Hollywood and becomes a movie star Tanya Clare the sex goddess of the Depression era famous from coast to coast and even in a strange desert area east of Hollywood where unknown to anyone in a wasteland of shacks and gullies another branch of the family survives the offspring of the outlaw Tomás after he went into the hills and joined up with the surviving members of the Harrowers establishing a withdrawn deeply religious community dirt-poor and nurturing apocalyptic ideas a branch that might have passed into oblivion had not old Tomás now blind and half-cracked related in fragments to little grandson Luke the story of the family the murders and disasters the crimes and curses that befell them a story so impressive it marks Luke for life causing him to grow up discontented and restless and unable to fit into the grim austerity of the community falling by consequence into the life of a drifter for whom the family's tradition is like a subterranean stream inside him even as outwardly he's succeeded in becoming nobody a person abandoned by history who goes from town to town and in one town transforms himself into a gas station attendant until one sultry afternoon Tina the wild young daughter of the local judge drives into the gas station and everything happens in about five minutes they take the money from the till and drive around holding up stores all across the Southwest a course of action that feels natural to Luke since he's under a curse anyway because of the terrible past of his family as his grandfather told it to him and which he transmits in turn to the judge's daughter telling her we were put on earth to suffer and to cause suffering an attitude that makes him such a natural for the criminal life

that before too long he's mixed up with small-time gangsters and con artists and the money is getting better and
promises to get immeasurably better after they settle in
Hollywood and get involved in a scheme to blackmail a
movie star it seems the mother of the famous sex goddess
Tanya Clare committed a murder and if it leaks out even
though the mother is dead by now her career will be ru-
ined by the bad publicity and of course the story leaks out
because Tanya Clare is troubled by memories of her childhood what with having a crazy artist for a father and a vicious blackmailer for a stepfather she's subject to night-
marish bouts of anxiety and suspicion and will try anything to alleviate all these jagged feelings yoga drugs clair-
voyants her latest fad being a smooth-talking psychoana-
lyst who persuades her he has unique insight into her
problems and who gets her to spill the whole story of her
mother's crime under hypnosis without her even knowing
she's told him while meantime the doctor likes to gamble
and is up to his ears in debt to some bookies who've been
doing business with Luke and inadvertently put him in the
know unfortunately for them because once Luke has the
information he knows he's hit pay dirt and doesn't see any
reason why he should split the take with a couple of cut-
rate bookies so he arranges to have them killed by the wily
method of spreading a rumor that the bookies ratted on a
big-time racketeer in the Los Angeles area so that when a
third party bumps them off nobody even connects him
with their disappearance all of which goings on give Tina
the judge's daughter who is by now not quite so wild as she

used to be some qualms about Luke's activities so much so that she ends up running to the actress and telling her all about the hypnotist and the blackmail plot putting them both in such jeopardy they have no recourse but to flee together heading for the Midwest where a young guy they've taken into their confidence a talented tap dancer on contract to the studio has relatives on whose farm they can hide out except that Luke and his gangster friends find them even there and it turns into a chase across America a chase in the course of which Tina and the tap dancer begin to fall in love and Tanya Clare and Tina develop a kind of mother-daughter relationship and learn all sorts of things about themselves and about America meeting so many people in the course of their journey farmers waitresses schoolchildren a washed-up vaudevillian a worldly-wise carnival fortune-teller that they almost forget about why they're on the road and in fact it's only because they all get so chummy that one night Tina tells Tanya about Luke's family and their ancestral curse and Tanya grasps that he's descended from the other branch of the family that Luke's grandfather was her mother's cousin the outlaw everybody thought was lost forever in the American desert and the coincidence is so bizarre that they can't do much more than stare at each other in bewildered silence until the young tap dancer says why worry this is America nobody has to live under any such long-forgotten shadow let the dead past bury its dead and let's go to New York and start over again we'll make a clean break and it's all beginning to sound wonderful until Tina remembers Luke and the gangsters and realizes they'll always be living under a threat but the tap dancer smiles and pulling a newspaper clipping out of his wallet says not anymore it seems there was a shooting out Chicago way last week Luke and his gangster friends turned on each other after the collapse of the blackmailing scheme and in the end Luke was the last one left with one bullet in his gun and another lodged in his gut to settle his accounts with the hypnotist whom he finally cornered on an abandoned railroad bridge where they faced off and died clinging to each other as they tumbled toward the cataracts Luke letting out a howl of unreconciled hatred as he disappeared into the freezing water leaving the field open for Tina and Tanya Clare and the tap dancer to go to New York where Tanya Clare revitalizes her career doing Shakespeare on Broadway and Tina marries the tap dancer and they all settle in a little cottage in Larchmont Tanya having legally adopted Tina making her heir to whatever remains of the heirlooms handed down from the Visigoths a historical legacy that seems strangely apt when Tina's brilliant young son Luc so named in honor of a family that even though they were not strictly speaking bound to it by blood ties both Tina and the tap dancer felt was somehow the font and origin of all their fortune in life retraces the ancient route of the family in the course of his long career as diplomat and strategist infiltrating the secret worlds of postwar Europe and ultimately playing a crucial role in the global conflicts of the Cold War era indeed by some accounts almost single-handedly averting another world war even if no public honor could ever acknowledge the fact but for him and those who loved him the best medal was that same Visigothic necklace passed on through the generations bestowed by Tanya Clare the last of the line whose portrait framed above the mantelpiece in the Larchmont home testified to the almost saintly austerity of her final years the necklace that he now held in hand as testimony that the blasphemies of the past were ready to dissolve finally in the unending fulfillment of a future he was only beginning to imagine a future in which his ancient family freed from its curse would go about the simple business of living with a new zest an appreciation of small things an enduring affection for those tiny gestures and private phrases with which they communicated to one another their willingness simply to endure and continue to the next chapter of a story that could never really end not even in the farthest reaches of space coursing across galaxies as yet unnamed not even in those centuries down which that jeweled necklace would continue to be passed would there be anything that could be called a conclusion and to grasp that was curiously like staring into an empty space a space that might have existed simply to frame the gem-encrusted necklace he cradled lovingly in his palm and that was old when the French Revolution was young a space that appeared to recede before him like a promise that was best honored by not being kept as he turned abruptly and passed with a resigned air into the adjoining kitchen and through a screen door into the glittering haze of the garden beyond.

A Meditation on Reading

And then he put down the book he had been reading, he –

But of course it was I, not he. Nevertheless, I had exercised the greatest care to read it as he would have done. At no point did I know him better than when reading as if through his eyes, weighing the words on his terms with a secret relief that it was not me doing the weighing. The words were transformed. It was his "coast" and his "scandals" and his "shadow": they were made foreign things, transformed by imagining his sharp dry glance. The world broke apart into interestingly separate pieces. There was my "shadow" and his "shadow" and there was, presumably, just plain "shadow" – hard to think of but so tantalizing in its aloofness, a word that didn't belong to anyone, a word that existed by itself. A reader without a shadow would be a vampire. What manner of entity would "shadow" be without a reader?

Somewhere in the depths of that library I lose track of Doctor Tobacco. He disappears into the silence whose definition was the cause of his imprisonment. All that remains of the latter end of his life are the books he read.

The Voice in the Well

Bᴜᴛ ᴡʜᴏ ᴄᴏᴜʟᴅ ʜᴀᴠᴇ ᴡʀɪᴛᴛᴇɴ such a treatise, if not him? This question bothered me for some time, and gave me cause to recollect a good many scattered threads of my earlier life and reading. Somewhere, it seemed, I had gotten an inkling of just such a series of propositions. At length I remembered where: did not this little pamphlet carry the inflections of the deacon's daughter, the author of that lost manuscript of poetry that I pried once, I seem to recollect, from under the floorboards? I have forgotten by now the exact purport of those poems but retain a sense of texture, the memory of a cadence that is like a sustaining atmosphere. I live in the memory of it.

The underlying tone, a sort of involuntary parody of the worst excesses of medieval scholasticism, should have tipped me off. How attentively she had absorbed her father's pedantic scholarship in order to fill out the world in which her allegorical figures moved and had their being. Who indeed could have written it better than she who had (I remember from her diaries) done little in her invalid's life but read, read in the window seat, read on the bench in the garden, read on the sofa, read at the thick oak table, read in bed as the morning light flooded the room, as the rain dragged on endlessly all afternoon, by candlelight in the middle of the night when the silence in the house was so intense that it could truly be said that the book was all that spoke, the only voice in the world?

I come back to such a voice, as if there were only one, the voice of what narrates and of which the narrators are transient vehicles: the voice (nearly audible) in the silent house where I sit up all night reading this book, these books, these shreds and tags and slivers of books. The voice is not of any particular person, although (like a playwright trying out his new manuscript) it assumes all the roles: voices of the blind and the mad, kings in broken halls, gross drunkards and nimble-tongued swindlers, seers and fools, nuns and toddlers.

Beneath them all is a voice that seems to come from underground or from within a sealed tower, like the voice of Semiramis in Calderón's play *La hija del aire.* She has been sequestered to spare the world the miseries predicted for her eventual reign as empress of Babylon. By the sheer force of her complaint – "if you do not suspend the laws of this prison where I am buried alive, I will put myself to death this very day" – the prison is opened, she rises into air and sunlight:

> In vain you try to make me obey you,
> today is the day when my ambition
> must break through the limits of your strictures.
> Even if I were dealt two thousand blows
> I would not go back into that sepulchre . . .
> If I die let it be from the lightning
> and not merely from the thunder.

She wants to live. Only through language can she reach the light. As she surfaces, history begins.

Yet she was only a character in a play by Calderón, just as Doctor Tobacco was, in the final analysis, a character in the poem by the deacon's daughter, nothing but a fantasy woven around the absurd name that popped into her head in the aftermath of a peculiar dream. The pages of description she lavished on him – his crinkled and faded possessions, the peculiar light that gleamed in his eyes, the habitual rhythms of his comings and goings by which the local people could tell the time, the legends they concocted about his supposed gifts of fortune-telling and healing – stemmed solely from the long hours she was compelled to spend staring out her window at the unchanging landscape. The Doctor was nothing more than a decorative element, one of the many with which her beautiful text was studded.

If only I could find a copy of it. If only I had not mislaid it, or had paid closer attention to the physical location of

that house, those floorboards. It is strange to be haunted by
the memory of words that one cannot quite remember. So
many sentences in so many books seem troubling reminders
of that other book I have no hope of ever again holding.

There is that which is unwilling to be nailed down, that
which will not, in Poe's words, "permit itself to be read."
(This was the same Poe who affirmed that "indefiniteness is
an element of the true music," the saint of browsers whose
stories were not complete without arcane and sometimes
manufactured quotations from the lyrics of Béranger, the
drama of Crébillon, the "Amatory Poems" of Don Thomas
De Las Torres or "those mystical writings which are usually
considered the mere dross of the early German literature.")
Knowledge, beyond a certain point, will not help. An accurate assessment of when and where and toward what end all
these books were written would not account for the peculiar
shiver a person might experience while reading them. The
shiver, strictly speaking, has nothing at all to do with the
book: but isn't it the book's only real excuse for taking up
space? I begin by reading against history and end up feeling
that I'm reading against language itself. In the very heart of
change, in the tumultuous unsalvageable river of speech,
I'm looking for what doesn't change .

What could I have been hoping for? To come upon the
blank page that is full of meaning, the place toward which
the sentences converge? That white book that would indeed

be like the lover for whom the reader had waited a lifetime? To read past its proem, its preface, would that not be like an almost infinitely slow undressing, the eye going down the page as if down the body of the beloved, the mind advancing through the evolutions of syntax as if through the grammar of desire, moving through language to be rid of language, shedding sentence after sentence, coiling through the whorls of structure and word bonding, the splitting off of parts of speech, while the still-wet glue of grammar slides and wobbles to admit interpolation and reversal and contradiction, the letters somersaulting in and out of one another, the sentence consenting to be torn apart, learning to inhabit a chaos that is a calligraphy, a calligraphy that is a mess of smeared thatching and rainslick flicker, to find beyond the last full stop a tabula rasa where silence grows wild?

It is some kind of silence I have arrived at by dint of sitting here under the light of a bare bulb surrounded by darkness.

Through immersion in books I arrive at a place beyond books, where reading navigates the variations of an interminable inner chant: The book is moss. The book is dross. The book is flake. The book is plate. The book is break. The book is flute. The book is hook. The book is quake. The book is crack. The book is crate. The book is bay. The book is key. The book is shell. The book is shake. The book is bell. The book is growl. The book is furl. The book is flume. The book is palm. The book is plain. The book is claim. The book is chain. The book is clamp. The book is perch. The book is rail. The book is torch. The book is squeal. The book is snort. The book is court. The book is curb. The book is cask. The book is curse. The book is swerve. The book is wave. The book is foam. The book is moan. The book is hem. The book is swim. The book is term. The book is form. The book is farm. The book is swarm.

At this point, none too soon, the sun has started to come up. Light leaks into the warehouse and I can at last click off the light that has been my guide and companion during these hours.

The Other Side of the Garden

CLOTHES DAMP, chilled to the bone, I am nonetheless cheered, as if mere sunlight were enough to dissipate the weight of what the night had accumulated. Only now can I begin to get a sense of what the bushes and bears that haunted my reading really were.

Who was I, after all, before I started reading? Does it matter, since from the moment I started on that path I became the creature of these pages? The reader strips himself of everything except the capacity to read. Naked, he is reborn in whatever world he has chosen. Or has it chosen him?

This is perhaps the mere exhaustion of one who has been filled and emptied and will be filled again, and emptied again. What is the reader without his book? A suspended lute waiting for something to pluck it, waiting to resound.

I tried to tell them, earlier, in that room, only they couldn't hear because they no longer had ears. I could hear them with excellent clarity but to reply was difficult, in fact impossible. I have the last word but it does me little good.

A Meditation on Reading

The reader, finally, is this mute creature into whom the words come bearing their final message.

Did I in fact read something, in the end, or did I never quite begin, never quite engage with all those promises, those shadows extending a hint of concealed depths? I have hovered near the beginnings. Having shed what I am in order to be absorbed into what I was about to read, did I spend all night caught between two states, no longer myself and not yet fully entered into that other universe, the one that begins with the next sentence?

IT BEGINS ANYWHERE. Here's one, for instance. It's a sort of novel. There is a picture of a house on the cover. The characters seem to be rather young. They've gathered somewhere; it's a vacation, or a reunion. Perhaps someone has died. Perhaps they have been summoned to the reading of a will. Or it might be the commemoration of an event in which they all participated some years back, and now they will begin to register how much they have changed in the meantime. In any event, they seem to have plenty of time on their hands. Old currents still move beneath the civilized surface of their conversation. There are whispers of passions, jealousies, fits of depression, abortions, suicide attempts.

It all seems awfully familiar. I wonder if I haven't read it before, or even if I haven't in truth been reading this same book forever, all my life, as if it were the only book.

The Browser's Ecstasy

I know this place. There used to be a room down the hall with heaps of books in it. It was on the other side of the garden. As I walk along the path in the twilight, I hear voices raised in energetic conversation. There must be at least ten or twelve people in there. I know them all, of course: the debonair Rex, with his unfailing charm and offhanded optimism; Marjorie, with whom I whiled away many an evening with talk of fictional characters who were like family to us; Phyllida, whose long, fraught silences had by contrast suggested that there were limits to what a book could convey.

— *Well, look who's here.*

It appears they know me too. I enter the room and find that only a few minutes have passed since I left. The smoke had grown so thick I needed some minutes in the garden to clear my head. During that brief absence they have already covered a fantastic range of subjects. They have skated from lamaism to mountain climbing, from Greek hecatombs to Spanish sherries, from the madness of Tasso to the angelic disposition of George Herbert, from sunrise on the Saguenay to the horrors of the black hole of Calcutta.

Here they find as much peace as they ever will, the slightly frantic peace of katydids and ice-skaters. They love to agree, they love to disagree, they love simply to reiterate the precise phrase that gave delight. They inhabit a fabric woven of words, a space more truly a home than those they periodically furnish or vacate. Within